S0-BUD-132

THE ESSENTIAL GUIDE TO ACCIDENT CASES IN WASHINGTON

Little Kids, BIG ACCIDENTS

What Every Parent Should Know About Children & Accidents

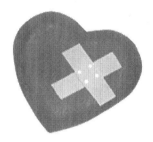

CHRISTOPHER M. DAVIS

Attorney at Law

Word Association Publishers
www.wordassociation.com

Copyright © 2008 by Christopher Michael Davis

All rights reserved. No part of this book may be reproduced, stored in a retrieval system, or transmitted by any means, electronic, mechanical, photocopying, recording, or otherwise, without written permission from the author.

Printed in the United States of America.

ISBN: 978-1-59571-334-6

Word Association Publishers
205 Fifth Avenue
Tarentum, Pennsylvania 15084
www.wordassociation.com

To

my wife, Anne Mischelle

my children, Hannah and Jackson

To say that my life without them would be far less fulfilling is an understatement. I love them all. I am especially grateful to my wife, who helped me write this book and who offered suggestions that greatly improved it.

CONTENTS

DISCLAIMER

The information in this book is just that—INFORMATION. This book does not constitute legal advice, and no attorney-client relationship has been formed by receiving and reading this book. Although the author is a licensed attorney in good standing in the state of Washington, Mr. Davis is not the reader's attorney, nor is he the attorney for an injured child, absent a signed retainer agreement (as required by Washington State's attorney ethics rules).

Many cases resulting from serious injuries to children involve complex legal issues or questions where the outcomes are heavily, if not completely, influenced by the individual facts of the case. Therefore, for specific legal advice, it is advisable to consult with an attorney who has experience representing the interests of children in injury claims. Anyone who wishes to consult with Mr. Davis about a specific case can find his contact information at the back of this book.

INTRODUCTION

As a lawyer who has tried many accident cases, I have found the most tragic and heart-wrenching ones to be those involving children. As a father, I find these cases personally difficult to manage. No parent wants to see any child suffer, but especially his or her own, and particularly when the injury was preventable. And these cases can be difficult to pursue in the legal arena.

Most of the time the adversary is a powerful insurance company that is willing to bankroll an aggressive and time-consuming defense (even when the case involves a seriously injured child). When a child has been seriously injured, the parents are often both angry and sad, sometimes filled with guilt, and overwhelmed by the legal process that may ensue. It is therefore often wise to hire a lawyer, and the lawyer should be one with experience in child injury cases.

I see many different types of accident cases involving chidren. These include:

- Auto accidents
- Boating accidents
- Motorcycle accidents
- Bicycles, scooters, and skateboard injuries
- Animal and dog bites
- School bus accidents
- School playground injuries
- Premises injuries
- Trampoline injuries
- Swimming pool accidents or drowning
- Snow ski injuries
- Amusement park injuries
- Burn injuries
- Summer camp injuries
- School or daycare injuries

- Birth injuries
- Auto back-over accidents
- Window fall injuries
- Swing set or play equipment injuries
- Defective or dangerous toys
- Food poisoning
- Medical malpractice injuries
- Sports injuries
- Bullying or assault cases

I wrote this book for two reasons: first, to create awareness about the most common injury accidents involving children, so that parents and family members can take appropriate precautions to avoid them, and second, to offer some knowledge and comfort to those parents who find themselves in the awful position of having a child who has been seriously injured due to someone's negligence or carelessness.

—Christopher M. Davis
September 2008

Chapter One

Basic Facts: Children and Accidents

Auto Accidents

By far the most common type of injury accident involving children is one that also involves a motor vehicle collision. According to the National Center for Statistics and Analysis (NCSA), nearly 250,000 children are injured every year in car accidents. This means that on any given day nearly 700 children are harmed due to accidents on our roadways. Of the 250,000 kids injured each year, approximately 2,000 die from their injuries. Children make up about 5% of total fatalities due to car accidents. In fact, for children between the ages of 2 and 14, motor vehicle accidents are the leading cause of death. Car accidents are also the leading cause of acquired disability (e.g., brain injury, paralysis) for children nationwide. And approximately 20% of the children who die in a car accident each year are killed in accidents involving a driver who is legally intoxicated. Nearly half of these children were killed while riding as passengers in an automobile driven by an intoxicated driver.

The failure of a child to wear a seat belt or use a safety seat is a contributing factor in more than half of the cases involving children who die in car accidents. Not only is an unrestrained child a potential distraction to the driver of the vehicle, but also the failure to wear a seat belt dramatically increases the chance that a child will suffer much more serious injury or death.

According to the National Highway Traffic Safety Administration (NHTSA), at least 72% of the 3,500 observed vehicle safety restraints for children were being used incorrectly.

When that happens, the risk that the child will suffer an injury or more severe injury rises even more. NHTSA estimates that a properly installed and used child safety seat lowers a child's risk of death by 71% for infants and by 54% for toddlers ages 1 to 4.

Every state, including Washington, requires the use of approved child safety seats for children under the age of 5. According to NCSA there is only a 90% compliance rate with respect to using approved safety seats for children under this age. The Washington State Patrol (WSP) recommends that for children who are under one year of age or who weigh less than 20 pounds, the parents should follow the guidelines of the American Academy of Pediatrics (AAP) by seating the child facing the rear of the vehicle. Children who are ages 1 to 4 and weigh 20 to 40 pounds can sit facing the front of the vehicle. Children between the ages of 4 and 8, or who are no taller than 4'9", are required by Washington law to use booster seats (including lap and harness belts). The WSP recommends that the booster seat also meet AAP guidelines. The child restraint system must be used properly according to the instructions provided by both the seat AND vehicle manufacturer.

The WSP also recommends that an approved booster seat be used if: (1) the child's knees do not otherwise bend comfortably at the edge of the seat, (2) the child does not sit with his/her hips all the way against the back of the auto seat, (3) the lap belt does not lie on top of the child's thighs, (4) the shoulder harness is not centered on the child's shoulder and chest, or (5) the child cannot stay seated under the above conditions during the entire trip.

Notably, a recent study found that a key factor influencing the increased risk of harm to children in accidents is moving the child prematurely from a child restraint system up to an adult seat and then allowing the child to sit in the front seat too soon.[1]

---

1. *Partners for Child Passenger Safety Fact and Trend Report, 2006.*

Parents can visit the Web site of the Washington State Safety Restraint Coalition at *www.800buckleup.org* to check out the current *Buyer's Guide to Child Car Seats and Booster Seats.*

Washington law also requires that children under the age of 13 must sit in the back seat of the vehicle "when it is practical to do so." Presumably, this means that a child under age 13 must sit in the back seat if it is reasonably possible to do so. AAP guidelines also recommend that children under the age of 13 sit in the back seat regardless of whether or not the vehicle is equipped with a passenger-side air bag. The age of 13 may appear to be an arbitrary figure, but studies show that most children at this age are still smaller than the average adult. So to reduce the risk of serious injury, it makes sense that the law requires children under this age to sit in the rear of the vehicle.

Interestingly, children are not required to wear seat belts while riding on a school bus. The NHTSA has determined that school buses already have "built-in protection" for children based on the special construction and size of bus seats, so that seat belt restraints are unnecessary. However, school bus crashes occurring at speeds greater than 35 mph still pose a serious risk of harm to children who are riding on the bus. There are certain precautions that, if exercised, can reduce the chance of serious injury in bus accidents. If your child's bus does not have safety belts, teach your child to ride near the front of the bus and to never stand in the bus while it is moving. Studies have also shown that two children riding on a bench seat have a lower risk of injury than three occupants riding in the same seat.

Schools should provide adequate adult supervision while children are boarding and exiting the bus. All bus stops should be located in safe locations that minimize the need for children to cross the street. Parents are well advised to trace their child's normal route to and from school while identifying potential danger spots and also to instruct the child about where to walk and cross the street.

Pedestrian Accidents

In cases involving children who die in traffic accidents, at least 30% involve children under the age of 15 who are pedestrians. Pedestrians account for about 30% of all traffic fatalities involving children under the age of 15 years. NHTSA estimates that more than one-fifth (22%) of children between the ages of 5 and 9 who were killed in traffic crashes were pedestrians. Approximately 19% of children involved in traffic fatalities under age 16 were pedestrians. And approximately 8% of all children under age 16 injured in a car accident were pedestrians. Forty-five percent of all pedestrian fatalities involving children under age 16 were killed between 3:00 PM and 7:00 PM. In Washington State alone, of the total number of children who die every year in car accidents, between 10 and 15 are pedestrians.[2]

---

2. Washington Traffic Safety Commission, Traffic Safety Date for years 1993-2003.

Studies have shown that by age 3, boys outnumber girls in pedestrian nonfatal injuries and in pedestrian fatality accidents by a margin of almost 2 to 1.[3] Many of the injuries to toddlers and preschoolers are considered "non-traffic," namely, these accidents mostly occur in places like driveways and parking lots instead of public roadways or thoroughfares. Nearly half of all pedestrian accidents involving children ages 1 to 4 occur when a vehicle is backing up in the driveway. According to a national advocacy organization, *Kids and Cars* (www.kidsandcars.org), approximately 50 children are injured or killed every week as a result of a vehicle backing up. The number of back-over deaths has actually increased in recent years. From 2002 through 2006, there were 474 children who died, compared with 128 deaths reported during the period from 1997 to 2001. Research has shown that children in this age range are simply too young to understand the dangers posed by a moving vehicle.

To combat the rising death toll of children in back-over accidents, Congress recently enacted the Cameron Gulbransen Act.[4] The act was named for a two-year-old who was killed when he was inadvertently backed over by a SUV because the vehicle's blind spot made it virtually impossible for the driver to see him. The act directs the United States Department of Transportation to adopt new safety standards that will lead to the design and development of safety technologies to prevent injury and death to children caused by back-over accidents and will result in safeguards that will become standard equipment in all vehicles.

The risks for school-age children of getting hit by a moving vehicle are different from those for toddlers. Children under the age of 10 still need supervision when crossing the street. Oftentimes a school-age child will forget about vehicles traveling in the street and dart out suddenly and without warning. Many pedestrian accidents involving school-age children (ages 6 to 11) occur in the morning and afternoon, and at times when children

---

3. *Pedestrian Injuries to Young Children* by Lynn Walton-Haynes, DDS, MPH (2002).
4. H.R. 1216—110th Congress (2007), Cameron Gulbransen Kids Transportation Safety Act of 2007 (also called K.T. Safety Act of 2007).

are typically at play.

The financial consequences of a child pedestrian accident can be significant as well. In 1999, the average hospital stay for a pedestrian accident was two days and the cost was more than $25,000.[5] These figures were compiled from statistics nearly 10 years ago; undoubtedly, the average hospital medical charge for a typical pedestrian accident is much higher today. Nearly one-third (32%) of the accidents involved injuries to the lower legs, most often fractures (87%). About 25% of pedestrian nonfatal accidents involved hospitalization for traumatic brain injury (TBI).

Most child pedestrian accidents are preventable. Parents need to be educated about the developmental limitations of their children in understanding the dangers of a moving vehicle. Parents can also teach younger children about the dangers of playing near the roadway or when it is appropriate to cross the street. There are also ways to minimize danger by creating safer roads and street crossings, especially near schools, playgrounds, and other areas where children congregate. And finally, law enforcement can play a pivotal role by diligently enforcing traffic laws in areas where children are active and by making drivers aware of pedestrian crossings.

Bicycle Accidents

Other than automobiles, bicycles are associated with more childhood injuries than any other consumer product. More than 70% of children ages 5 to 14 (27.7 million) ride bicycles. This age group rides 50% more than the average cyclist, accounting for 21% of all bicycle-related deaths and nearly 50% of all bicycle-related injuries. More than 130 children die every year in bicycle accidents and approximately 270,000 are treated in

---

5. *Pedestrian Injuries to Young Children* by Lynn Walton-Haynes, DDS, MPH (2002).

emergency rooms for injuries.[6] Nearly half of these children sustain a traumatic brain injury because of their failure to wear a helmet-or to wear a safe and properly fitted helmet.

Studies have shown that a properly fitted helmet can reduce the risk of bicycle-related brain injuries by as much as 88%. Properly fitted bike helmets can prevent an estimated 75% of fatal head injuries to children each year. Motor vehicles are involved in approximately 90% of the fatal bike crashes that happen each year. About 60% of child fatalities in bike-versus-auto crashes occur on residential streets. A child who does not wear a helmet is fourteen times more likely to suffer a fatal crash than one who does. Clearly, the chances of injury and/or death decrease dramatically when a child wears a protective helmet while riding a bicycle.

Dog Bites

According to the Centers for Disease Control and Prevention (CDC), an estimated 68 million dogs are kept as pets in the United States. More than one million dog bites are reported each year. And there are estimates that an equal number of dog bites (one million) go unreported each year. Of the one million or so dog bites reported each year, about 60% involve an injury to a child. Approximately 70% of dog bite wounds are inflicted on the child's face. Children ages 5 to 9 have the highest dog-bite-related injuries.

More than 60% of dog bites occur in the home of the dog owner. Approximately 77% of dog bite victims are members or close friends of the dog owner's family and are therefore familiar with the dog.

Contrary to popular myth, there is no such thing as a child-friendly dog breed. Although some breeds may be more suitable for children, a dog's propensity to bite is dependent on many factors, including the dog's inherited traits, environment,

---

6. Safe Kids USA (www.safekids.org).

training, and socialization. Studies have shown that the most positive influence on a dog's comfort around children is positive interaction with children when the dog is a young puppy.

There are some guidelines that, if followed, can reduce the chance that a dog will bite a young child. The critical age for socializing a dog is between the ages of 3 and 14 weeks. A dog in this age range that is introduced to young children has a much lower incidence rate of biting kids. Also, neutering male dogs decreases the chance of aggressive behavior.

If you plan to have young children and a dog, it is best to adopt the dog while it is young and introduce it to the children during the toddler age. However, dogs need to be introduced to children of all ages. Young toddlers will act differently around the dog than a 10-year-old child will. Children should be involved with the training sessions of the dog. This allows the dog to experience the child as an authoritative figure, thereby decreasing the chances that the dog will bite the child. Children should also be involved in other caretaking activities, like feeding, grooming, and bathing the dog.

Parents should never leave young children alone with a dog, particularly if the dog has limited experience with that child. You can teach children to recognize fearful or aggressive behavior in a dog so they can take steps to avoid or minimize the risk of a bite. And finally, parents should set good examples of how to treat the dog. Children tend to emulate their parents' behavior, which would include the parents' interaction with the dog.

Playground Injuries

The CDC reports that more than 200,000 children ages 14 and younger are treated at emergency rooms each year for playground-related injuries. About 45% of injuries on playgrounds are severe (i.e., fractures, internal injuries, concussions, dislocations, and amputations). About 75% of nonfatal accidents occur on public playgrounds, with most occurring at schools and daycare centers. Between 1990 and

2000, there were 147 deaths of children at or under the age of 14. Fifty-six percent of these deaths were caused by strangulation and 31% occurred due to falls onto the playground surface. Most of the deaths (70%) occurred in home play areas.

While all children are at risk for injury on playgrounds, girls are at more at risk (55%) when compared with boys (45%). Children between the ages of 5 and 9 have the highest rate of emergency room visits of any age group. Studies have shown that more injuries on public playgrounds occur on climbing equipment than any other type. On playgrounds at private residences, the swing or swing set is the most common cause of injury. One study found that more injuries occur on playgrounds located in low-income areas due to infrequent and/or inadequate maintenance of equipment.[7] Parents need to make sure that their child is familiar with the equipment on the playground. Close supervision, at least initially, may also be a good idea before children are allowed to play at a specific playground.

Swimming and Water Accidents

The CDC reports that there are on average nearly 10 drowning accidents occurring every day. More than one in four fatal drowning accidents involve children ages 14 and younger. For every child who drowns, there are at least 4 others who visit the emergency room for nonfatal submersion injuries. Nonfatal drowning injuries can be catastrophic and can cause permanent brain damage, including problems with learning and memory, and the permanent loss of brain function.

Children under the age of 5 are at the greatest risk of near-drowning because their energy and curiosity can easily lead them to fall into bodies of water, including bathtubs or large buckets from which they cannot escape. Among children ages 1 to 4 who die in accidents, nearly 30% do so through unintentional

---

7. Suecoff SA, Avner JR, Chou KJ, Crain EF. A Comparison of New York City Playground Hazards in High- and Low-Income Areas. *Archives of Pediatrics & Adolescent Medicine* 1999;153:363-6.

drowning. Fatal drowning is the second leading cause of unintentional injury-related death for children ages 1 to 14. Children under 1 year of age most often drown in bathtubs, buckets, or toilets. With children between the ages of 1 and 4, most drowning incidents occur in swimming pools. Most young children who drown in swimming pools were last seen in the home, had been out of sight for less than five minutes, and were in the care of one or both parents at the time.

There are certain risk factors that exist for fatal and nonfatal drowning accidents. A major risk factor is the absence of pool barriers; another is the absence of parental supervision. Most pool accidents involving children occur within minutes after the child is last seen alive. Many pool incidents occur because the child has easy access to the water. Drowning incidents that occur in natural settings like lakes, rivers, and oceans increase with the child's age.

Parents can take certain steps to minimize the risk of a drowning incident. The most important step is to provide adequate adult supervision. Parents should keep their child in view at all times when the child is around water. While supervising children, a parent should also avoid engaging in distracting activities, like reading, watching television, playing cards, doing yard work, etc. Barriers should be erected around swimming pools or other large bodies of water. Pool owners are in fact required by law to fence in their pools. A child should not be allowed to access the water without an adult's assistance. Parents should also teach their children to swim. Introducing small children to the water through swimming lessons is an extremely good idea. Do not let children use improper inflatable devices without direct supervision. Toys like "water wings," "noodles," and "inner tubes" are not designed to keep swimmers safe. These toys can give a child a false sense of security, thereby encouraging the child to take greater risks (e.g., venturing out into deeper water).

Household Accidents

Home injuries are one of the top reasons why children under the age of 3 years visit the emergency room. Nearly 70% of children who die at home from unintentional injuries are age 4 and younger. Young children have the highest risk of being injured at home because that is where they spend most of their time. Examples of these types of accidents include falling down stairs, ingesting poisonous substances, getting electrical shocks or burns, and being subject to cuts or amputations from playing with sharp or dangerous objects.

Medical Malpractice

Children who are victims of medical malpractice often suffer significant injury or death during the birthing process. Birth injuries are generally caused by something that went wrong during pregnancy or delivery, while birth defects are harms to the child that usually arose prior to birth and were often caused by genetic abnormalities or infection during pregnancy. Some studies have shown that birth injuries occur in five out of a thousand births (0.5%). Most birth injuries occur when a doctor, nurse, or midwife fails to adequately assess or respond to conditions that occur during pregnancy and/or delivery.

To pursue a medical negligence claim for harms suffered by a child, the injuries usually have to be severe if not catastrophic. This is because it takes enormous resources and expense to pursue the claim. Experts have to be hired to review the records and testify that the child suffered harm because the treating physician or other healthcare professional violated the standard of care. The cost of bringing a medical negligence claim can sometimes exceed six figures. In some cases, the cost can go as high as $500,000.[8]

8. The "cost" of bringing the case refers only to the costs of litigation, such as hiring experts, obtaining records, conducting depositions, creating exhibits, etc. This excludes the fees owed to the lawyer for his or her time and expertise. Most lawyers however are hired on a contingency fee in birth injury cases.

Medical negligence cases involving children include death, permanent brain damage, cerebral palsy, Erb's Palsy, and shoulder dystocia. Because medical negligence cases are often settled or resolved confidentially, there is no reliable database to show the actual number of children who are victims of medical negligence. Many times the negligence goes unreported due to the parents' unawareness and/or because the child's injuries are less than catastrophic or severe.

These are just a few categories of accidents that involve children. Of course, there are many others-too many to include in this book. What should be apparent, however, is that children face many different types of risks that can cause serious injury or even death. Parents should be aware of these risks so that proper precautions can be taken to protect their children. Many risks can be drastically reduced or even eliminated just by teaching parents and their children about injury prevention devices, like seatbelts and helmets. Other risks of harm can be lowered by properly supervising children and teaching them to watch out for certain risks such as moving vehicles, aggressive dogs, and hazards located inside the home.

Chapter Two

Important Legal Ramifications in Child Injury Cases

Does a Legal Claim Exist?

A child may have a legal claim arising from an injury accident. A legal claim arises when the child is entitled to compensation for the injuries and damages proximately caused by the accident. Whether a child has a legal claim for injuries sustained in an accident will depend on many different factors. Generally, a child will only have a legal right to recover compensation if the injuries were caused by another party's negligence. In Washington, the term "negligence" is defined as a person's failure to exercise "ordinary care," or the kind of care that would be deemed appropriate in the particular situation that led to the child's injury. Not only can a person be found negligent, but so can a corporation or governmental agency.

Oftentimes it is easy to determine whether a party was negligent, such as when a driver runs a stop sign or fails to yield to pedestrians in a crosswalk. The violation of a known rule, statute, or regulation can also provide evidence of a party's negligence. For example, if a person injures a child and also violates a statute or regulation while doing so, that violation may be admissible in a subsequent trial to prove that the person was negligent.

Sometimes there may be more than one negligent party who has caused the harm to the child. Washington follows the law of comparative negligence (also called comparative fault). This term means that more than one party may be responsible for a child's damages according to each party's percentage of negligence. For example, let's say Party A and Party B both negligently injured a child and that the child's damages were calculated at $100,000. Party A was found 25% responsible and Party B, 75%. Party A's share of the child's damages is $25,000 and Party B's share is $75,000. Under the law of comparative fault, each negligent party is only responsible for its share of damages as determined by the jury-or a judge, if the matter is tried without a jury (i.e., bench trial).

Joint and Several Liability

In Washington, there is an exception to the rule of comparative fault. That exception occurs when the injured child is considered fault-free, i.e., when it is determined that the child is not at fault. In that situation, if there are multiple negligent parties who have caused injury to the child, each of them will be jointly and severally liable for all damages. This means that each negligent party is responsible not only for his or respective share of fault, but is also individually responsible for 100% of the damages. Take the example of Party A and Party B above. If joint and several liability exists, then Party A will be responsible not only for its proportionate share of $25,000 but also for the full amount of damages calculated at $100,000. This holds true for Party B, who will be responsible not just for its proportionate share of $75,000 but also for the full $100,000 award.

Some people question whether the law of joint and several liability is fair. Sometimes a negligent party that shares a very small percentage of fault is legally required to pay a much higher percentage of the child's damages. For example, if Party A was only found to be 1% at fault and Party B 99% at fault, Party A owes $1,000 and Party B owes $99,000. Let's say Party B is uninsured and has no money to pay a verdict. Under the law of joint and several liability, Party A is still liable for the full $100,000. Is this fair? Well, the rationale behind joint and several liability is that it is more just to fully compensate an innocent victim than to allow a negligent party to limit his or her share of damages to that person's proportionate share of fault. Other commentators have noted that joint and several liability benefits society by effectively placing the economic burden on those who can afford it most (e.g., corporations, governmental entities, insurance companies) while at the same time protecting the innocent victim.[9]

Negligence of the Child

Washington's law of comparative negligence means that the proportionate share of fault of *all* potential negligent parties must be considered, even if it involves the conduct of a child. This means a child can be held negligent and therefore wholly or partially responsible for that child's injuries and damages. In Washington, the issue of the child's degree of negligence may also be called "contributory negligence." But there are certain limitations when it comes to accidents and injuries involving negligent children. First, the law in Washington is that children under the age of 6 years cannot be held negligent as a matter of law. The Washington State Supreme Court has decided that a child under age 6 does not have the mental capacity to be negligent.[10] This means that any time a child under age 6 has a legal claim for injuries caused by an accident, that child is deemed fault-free for purposes of deciding which parties negligently caused that child's injuries.

Children who are 6 years of age and older may be deemed negligent and thus legally responsible for their own injuries. But there is one important difference. In Washington, children are *not* to be judged by the same standards that apply to adults. We previously defined the negligence standard for adults as the failure to exercise ordinary care under the same or similar circumstances occurring at the time of the injury or the accident.

---

9. See Guido Calabresi & Jon T. Hirschoff, *Toward a Test for Strict Liability in Torts*, 81 YALE L.J. 1055 (1972).
10. *Price v. Kitsap Transit*, 125 Wn.2d 456, 886 P.2d 556 (1994).

For children, however, the negligence standard is defined much more narrowly. A child is negligent if that child fails to exercise the ordinary care that a "reasonably careful child of the same age, intelligence, maturity, training, and experience" would exercise under the same or similar circumstances. This is an important distinction. It means that a 7-year-old child cannot be judged according to the same standards that might apply to a 10-year-old child. The standard of negligence for children is also based heavily on the child's individual characteristics and traits. Conceivably, the actions of a special needs or mentally disabled child should only be judged based on the expected reasonable conduct by another child of the same age and/or intellectual capacity. The same goes for children who may be advanced or high functioning. High achieving children with excellent grades should only be judged based on the expected actions of other children similarly situated.

Parental Negligence and Parental Immunity

Usually when a child has been injured in an accident, the conduct of the child's parents is called into question. Typically the insurance company will try to argue that the child was injured in large part due to the parents' failure to adequately supervise the child. But this argument often fails. This is because Washington has adopted what is called the Parental Immunity Doctrine. Under this doctrine, a negligent parent is immune from liability for injuries caused to the child unless the parent was acting outside his or her parental capacity, or if the child's injuries were caused by a parent's willful and wanton misconduct. A parent is considered to be acting outside his or her parental capacity if the conduct is well beyond the bounds of appropriate parental parameters, such as conduct involving physical or sexual abuse. The Parental Immunity Doctrine is based upon the public policy of maintaining family tranquility and avoiding the fear of undermining parents' control and authority over their children.

An exception to the Parental Immunity Doctrine is when the child's injuries are due to a parent's negligent driving.[11] That means a child is still permitted to pursue a legal claim against his parent if the injuries arose from a car accident that was caused by the parent. The doctrine also does not apply to those parents who engage in willful and wanton misconduct. Washington law has defined the phrase "willful and wanton misconduct" to mean the parent's intentional act or intentional failure to act in disregard of a known peril or hazard. This can be a difficult burden to prove. While the standard of negligence implies inadvertence or carelessness, the term willfulness suggests premeditation or formed intention in the face of known circumstances that would inform a reasonable parent of the highly dangerous nature of that conduct. Essentially a parent's conduct must rise to the level of intentional or reckless conduct or extreme indifference that had a high likelihood to cause harm to the child.

The courts in Washington have rejected numerous attempts to hold a parent legally responsible for injuries caused to the child based on allegations of inadequate supervision. But in a recent case involving a stepparent, the Washington Supreme Court ruled that the stepparent could not be protected under the Parental Immunity Doctrine because that stepparent was not truly acting as a parent to the child. In that case, the stepparent fell asleep and the 3-year-old stepdaughter fell into the family swimming pool and drowned.[12] It turned out the stepparent had previously taken out a life insurance policy on the child, an unusual action by a stepparent, to say the least. Also, the stepparent had only recently married the child's mother, so there was a factual question of whether the stepparent had sufficient time to form a parent-child relationship and thus be entitled to the protection of the Parental Immunity Doctrine.

In another case the parents of a severely injured child were immune even though they were fully aware of the hazard that

---

11. *Merrick v. Sutterlin*, 93 Wn.2d 411, 610 P.2d 891 (1980).
12. *Zellmer v. Zellmer*, ___ Wn.2d ___ (July 24, 2008).

injured their child and had previously warned him to stay away from it.[13] In another case a father was held immune when his 3 year-old son was severely burned in a fire that the father had started in the backyard after which he left the child alone.[14] It is important to remember that the Parental Immunity Doctrine only protects negligent conduct in certain situations. A parent may still be legally and financially responsible for intentional conduct that harms the child, such as physical and sexual abuse.

Statute of Limitations

There are strict time limits on when a person may bring a legal claim arising from an injury accident. This is no different for claims brought by children. However, the general rule in Washington State is that a child has 3 years from the date of the child's 18th birthday to bring a claim.[15] This effectively means that the child can wait until his or her 21st birthday to settle the claim or file a lawsuit. It is usually not a good idea to wait this long to resolve the claim, especially if the case involves injuries to a younger child. However, certain exceptions may justify waiting until after the age of majority, depending on the facts of the claim.

Claims Against the Government

If a child has a claim against a governmental entity, such as a town, municipality, county, or state, certain requirements must first be met. A verified claim form must be served on the authorized agent for the governmental entity. Service of a valid claim form is a prerequisite to bringing a claim against the government. The name and address of the authorized agent who can accept service of the claim form is required to be kept as a

---

13. *Jenkins v. Snohomish Cy.* PUD 1, 105 Wn.2d 99, 713 P.2d 79 (1986).
14. *Talarico v. Foremost Ins. Co.*, 105 Wn.2d 114, 712 P.2d 294 (1986).
15. See RCW 4.16.190.

matter of public record with the auditor in the county in which the entity is located. With claims against the state of Washington, the agent who is authorized to accept service of the claim form is the state's Division of Risk Management in Olympia, Washington.

To be valid, the claim form must contain certain information. This information includes a description of the conduct and circumstances which brought about the injury or damage, a description of the injury or damage, the time and place the injury or damage occurred, the names of all persons involved, the residence of the claimant for a period of six months immediately before the claim arose, and a statement of the amount of damages claimed. A claim brought on behalf of a minor child can be verified and presented by the child's relative, attorney, or agent representing the child.

It is important to note that the content and service of the claim form must substantially comply with the requirements of the statute. Failure to substantially comply may result in the claim being denied and/or dismissed by a court of law. Once a claim form has been properly verified, presented, and served on the appropriate governmental entity, a period of 60 days must elapse before a lawsuit can be initiated. The failure to wait 60 days is a fatal mistake that will invalidate the claim and result in the dismissal of the case. The filing and presenting of claims against a governmental entity can be complex and confusing, so the claimant is wise to consult with or retain counsel.

Children Testifying in Court

If a lawsuit has been filed to recover financial compensation for a child's injuries, that child may be called to testify in court. However, most cases involving children never go to court. Therefore, the chances that a child will be forced to testify in court are extremely low.

The age of the child does not necessarily determine whether a child can or should testify. But in Washington, the admission of testimony by children under age 10 is within the discretion of the trial court.[16] Children under age 10 who appear incapable of understanding the subject matter or facts, or incapable of communicating information, may not be considered competent to testify.[17]

Generally, a child may be held competent to testify if that child (1) understands the obligation to speak the truth on the witness stand; (2) has the mental capacity, at the time of the occurrence concerning which the child is to testify, to receive an accurate impression of it; (3) has a memory sufficient to retain an independent recollection of the occurrence; (4) has the capacity to express in words a memory of the occurrence; and (5) has the capacity to understand simple questions about the occurrence. The final determination of whether the child is competent to testify will rest with the judge, who will evaluate and listen to the child, as well as consider the child's demeanor and manner of testifying.

Likelihood of Going to Court

Most child injury cases settle without going to court or trial. Statistically speaking, the chance that a typical personal injury case will go to trial is extremely small, probably less than 5% of all cases. The likelihood that a personal injury case involving a minor child will go to court is probably even smaller. In cases where the evidence of liability against the defendant is strong and the injuries are fairly serious, the likelihood of the case going to court will be even smaller.

Despite the low probability of a child injury case ever going to court, the case should nevertheless be thoroughly prepared as if it were going to trial. Insurance companies and their attorneys will not agree to pay a premium settlement offer unless they are convinced that there exists a strong possibility of a jury awarding much more money if the case were to go to trial. A case that has been competently and thoroughly prepared will therefore increase the likelihood that the case will settle short of trial.

16. See *Laudermilk v. Carpenter*, 78 Wn.2d 92, 102, 457 P.2d 1004 (1969).
17. See RCW 5.60.050(2).

Chapter Three

Dealing with the Insurance Company

In those cases where a child has been injured by a negligent party with insurance, the parents will at some point have to deal with the insurance company. Parents will need to address questions of liability and damages, including payment for past and future medical expenses and other damages incurred by the child. This can be a daunting and unsatisfying task. The parent of an injured child is likely already under a tremendous amount of stress, given the traumatic nature of the child's injury. Insurance adjustors are trained to take advantage of this fact so that the company can resolve or settle the claim as cheaply as possible.

First, a word about the insurance industry when it comes to resolving injury claims. It is fair to say that the moment a person has been injured by someone's negligence, that person has also entered into a war zone with the insurance industry. No, that is not an overstatement. For more than 30 years, the insurance industry has spent hundreds of millions, if not billions, of dollars on advertising to spread false and misleading information about accident claims. The industry wants people to believe that the justice system is out of control and that people who file lawsuits are getting millions of dollars for minor injuries. Take it from someone "in the trenches" who has settled and litigated hundreds, if not thousands, of injury claims: such propaganda simply isn't true. Oh sure, you will occasionally read in your local newspaper about a million-dollar settlement for what appears to be a minor injury, but such a case is usually the exception.

Most injury cases are resolved for amounts that are much less than a million dollars, and many times less than six figures. And this includes those cases involving more severe injuries. Many severe injuries receive inadequate or no compensation at all due to a variety of factors, not the least of which is the vigorous defense often mounted by the insurance company to either defeat the case entirely or to significantly lessen the value of the claim. The insurance carrier does this by hiring aggressive defense attorneys and high-priced experts to say that the accident was someone else's fault, that the injuries were not that severe, or that they were caused by some other factor or pre-existing condition. Most people have no idea about the extreme efforts some insurance carriers will make to defeat even legitimate claims. It is not uncommon for some of these companies to spend much more money defending the claim by hiring lawyers and experts than what they would spend to settle the case for a reasonable sum.

The insurance industry's far-reaching propaganda machine has created the false impression in the public's mind that the system needs fixing. Unfortunately, this campaign to disseminate "disinformation" has had an enormous negative influence on juries and their verdicts. Juries today are highly skeptical of people who file lawsuits that claim money for "pain and suffering" (even when those claims involve children!). Many people who wind up on juries believe the myths touted by the insurance industry, or they may be highly persuaded by the arguments of the insurance carrier's high-priced attorneys and the testimony of their formidable experts who earn substantial income working for the defense. These efforts by the industry may be a huge obstacle to achieving justice in the case of your child, even when the injuries are severe and the negligence of the other party has been conclusively established. Lawyers who handle injury cases have learned that it is much more difficult to achieve justice for their clients in today's climate of skepticism and heightened propaganda.

If your child has an injury claim, you need to be aware that the insurance adjustor will utilize any means necessary to pay out as little as possible, even on legitimate claims that involve serious injuries. It does not matter to the adjustor that the victim is a small child or that the injuries are so catastrophic as to evoke tremendous sympathy from people who understand what has happened to the child. Insurance claims adjustors receive extensive training on how to save the company money, and not necessarily on how to examine a child's claim fairly and pay a reasonable settlement. In fact, most insurance companies reward their claims adjustors with bonuses or promotions based on how much money these adjustors save the company rather than on whether the claims are settled fairly. So, when the adjustor listens to the facts of your child's injury claim, he or she is thinking of ways to pay out as little as possible so that the bonus is bigger at the end of the year.

Here are some of the tactics the adjustor will use to wear down injured claimants so they will accept much less money than what the claim is worth:

1. **Using delay tactics**. The adjustor is a master of using delay tactics to wear people down. He or she knows that many people (80-90%, according to some insurance company estimates) will grow tired of the delaying tactics and simply throw up their hands and say, "Enough!" These people will accept the low-ball offer just to be done with the entire unpleasant process.

2. **Requesting unnecessary information**. Yes, it's true that the insurance company will need records, receipts, bills, reports, and other documentation to support the claim. But sometimes the request for documentation is unnecessary-for example, asking for medical records from 10 years before the accident, or asking for tax returns from the same period. Such information typically is unnecessary and is only requested to delay resolution of the claim. Insurance adjustors know that repeated requests for unnecessary documentation can easily frustrate people and wear them down so they're more likely to accept a low settlement offer.

3. **Disputing the medical treatment**. Despite the absence of any medical training, the adjustor may question the need for treatment or certain procedures or worse: second-guess your own

doctor. Many times it does not matter to the adjustor that your treatment has been recommended by a reputable licensed physician.

4. **Disputing the medical charges**. Sometimes the adjustor will only agree to "accept" 70, 80, or 90% of your past medical charges. Again, such an assertion is made without having any medical background to support such a position. When "nickel and diming" the consumer, the well-trained adjustor knows that most people will not hire a lawyer to challenge the refusal to pay a small portion of the medical bills.

5. **Telling you not to hire an attorney**. Other times the insurance company will tell you that hiring an attorney is unnecessary. Sometimes the adjustor will try to prevent you from retaining an attorney by falsely stating that any settlement money you receive will go entirely to the attorney. Still, other times the adjustor may threaten to "deny" the claim if you hire a lawyer. If a claims representative tries to steer you away from retaining an attorney, this should be your first clue that using an attorney may actually produce a much higher recovery for you (even after deducting the attorney's fee).

6. **Misrepresenting insurance policy benefits**. Sometimes the adjustor will misrepresent the amount of insurance coverage that is available to you. Or worse, the adjustor won't tell you that the insurance coverage or certain types of benefits even exist. This tactic may be used to entice you into accepting a smaller settlement than what would otherwise be warranted.

7. **Acting as your friend**. There are times when the claims adjustor will "befriend" you and make it appear that he or she is watching out for your interests when in fact that is not the case. Sometimes the adjustor will give you advice about the type or frequency of your medical treatment, and then decide later on not to pay for the treatment because it is "excessive."

8. **Making false promises**. There are times when the adjustor will make promises to you that he or she knows can't be met. The adjustor's primary loyalty is to his/her employer (the insurance company) and to his/her insured (the negligent party).

Any adjustor who makes promises "for your benefit" inherently creates a conflict of interest. Oftentimes the adjustor already knows that a conflict is created by promising to protect your interests, but he/she knows this is one way to get you to lower your guard and get you to agree to terms that your attorney would never allow.

These are just a few of the tactics that the insurance industry will use to accomplish its goal of getting parents to accept smaller settlements for their injured children. Parents need to be aware that they are dealing with professional negotiators who strive to fulfill the insurance company's primary objective: to settle claims for much less than they are worth. Lower settlements mean bigger company profits. If parents begin to feel overwhelmed, they should not hesitate to consult with an attorney who has expertise in child injury claims.

Chapter Four

Children and Traumatic Brain Injury

Unfortunately, traumatic brain injury (TBI) is very common among children who are victims in accidents. According to the Centers for Disease Control, nearly one million children suffer a traumatic brain injury (TBI) each year.[18] More than 100,000 of these children require hospitalization. These figures probably underestimate the incident rate of TBI among children because many children never go to the hospital following the trauma and many TBI cases go undiagnosed due to a variety of factors. Also, many parents fail to initially recognize or appreciate some of the TBI symptoms in their children, resulting in a long delay from the time of injury to a firm diagnosis. Sometimes that diagnosis never comes if the child receives inadequate medical care.

Certain aspects of brain injury are unique to children and may have important legal ramifications when it comes to asserting and proving a claim for damages. Because I see a very high prevalence of brain injury among the many children my office represents, I am devoting an entire chapter to this type of injury claim. There are plenty of resources out there that will help parents understand the nature and treatment of TBI involving children. This chapter is not intended to provide an exhaustive resource on the subject of TBI when it comes to the diagnosis, treatment, and rehabilitation of TBI in children. Rather, it is an overview. I encourage parents to seek out other resources, including the National Brain Injury Association (www.biausa.org) and the Brain Injury Association of Washington (www.biawa.org).

---

18.   See also RCW 74.31.005.

What is TBI?

It is important to understand how TBI is defined. Recently the Washington state legislature adopted a law that defines "traumatic brain injury" as:

> ...injury to the brain caused by physical trauma resulting from, but not limited to, incidents involving motor vehicles, sporting events, falls, and physical assaults. Documentation of traumatic brain injury shall be based on adequate medical history, neurological examination, mental status testing, or neuropsychological evaluation. A traumatic brain injury shall be of sufficient severity to result in impairments in one or more of the following areas: cognition; language; memory; attention; reasoning; abstract thinking; judgment; problem solving; sensory, perceptual, and motor abilities; psychosocial behavior; physical functions; or information processing. The term does not apply to brain injuries that are congenital or degenerative, or to brain injuries induced by birth trauma. RCW 74.31.010(4).

This definition also mirrors the one adopted by the Individuals with Disabilities Education Act (IDEA) (formerly the Education of the Handicapped Act) and codified at 34 C.F.R. § 300.7(b)(12).

The Washington legislature has also recognized that TBI "can cause a wide range of functional changes affecting thinking, sensation, language, or emotions," and that the condition "can also cause epilepsy and increase the risk for conditions such as Alzheimer's disease, Parkinson's disease, and other brain disorders that become more prevalent with age." The legislature has further declared that "the impact of a traumatic brain injury on the individual and family can be devastating."[19]

It is encouraging that the state of Washington has formally recognized that a traumatic brain injury is a serious problem that

---

19. RCW 74.31.005.

can have long-lasting consequences for the individual victim and the victim's entire family. We have only recently begun to establish programs to help TBI survivors deal with this potentially devastating condition.

Degree of Injury: Mild, Moderate, or Severe TBI

The severity of TBI is typically categorized as a mild, moderate, or severe injury. These classifications, however, refer only to the initial traumatic insult along with the degree of neurological deficit. There is some disagreement among healthcare professionals about what factors must be present to support a particular classification. However, most experts agree that a severe TBI involves significant neurological deficits and a significant insult to the head or brain, like skull fracture or impalement. A moderate TBI may involve a lesser insult to the head or brain where fairly significant cognitive, physical, and psychosocial problems exist to varying degrees. The presence of seizures, severe headaches, and loss of consciousness (LOC) lasting several minutes, as well as loss of concentration and mental processing problems may also support a diagnosis of moderate TBI.

In the vast majority of cases a person will likely have suffered a mild TBI (MTBI). In fact, approximately 85% of TBI victims who claim compensation for brain damage will have sustained this level of injury. This is also true in my own practice, where most of my child TBI cases involve MTBI. But the label "mild TBI" is often a misnomer, because a "mild" brain injury can still cause significant disruption of a person's life. The MTBI Committee of the American Congress of Rehabilitation Medicine has defined MTBI as follows:

A patient with a mild traumatic brain injury is a person who has had a traumatically induced physiological disruption of brain function, as manifested by at least one of the following:

1. Any period of loss of consciousness;
2. Any loss of memory for a period of events immediately

before or after the accident;

    3.   Any alteration in mental state at the time of the accident (e.g., confusion, dazed feeling, disorientation); and

    4.   Focal neurological deficits that may or may not be transient, but where the severity of the brain injury does not exceed the following:

        a. LOC of approximately 30 minutes or less;

        b. After 30 minutes, an initial Glasgow Coma Scale of 13/15 (which may represent the person expressing some confusion, some inability to focus or follow commands, and/or speech problems);[20]

        c. Post-traumatic amnesia not greater than 24 hours.

Studies have shown that as many as 10-20% of MTBI patients may continue to experience long-term problems (lasting longer than 12 months following injury). However, there is disagreement among healthcare professionals about whether MTBI symptoms lasting longer than 12 months are actually due to the initial brain injury or to pre-existing factors, or a combination of both. In the legal setting involving MTBI claims, my experience has been that the insurance company and its attorneys and experts will almost always argue that MTBI symptoms lasting longer than 12 months are due solely to pre-existing factors or malingering, or both.

Does a Diagnosis of TBI Require Loss of Consciousness?

Insurance companies like to focus on whether the TBI victim has suffered a loss of consciousness (LOC) following the initial trauma. There is a common myth that a person must be rendered

---

20. The Glasgow Coma Scale is often used by hospitals to measure the level of consciousness vs. unconsciousness in a patient. The scale addresses 3 areas: eye response, motor response (arms and legs), and verbal response. A score of 15 is considered the highest and supports full consciousness. A score of 3 is the lowest and would suggest complete unconsciousness. A Glasgow Coma Scale rating of 15 does *not* rule out the existence of MTBI.

unconscious for a long period of time before a TBI can be sustained or diagnosed. The medical literature suggests that this is untrue. Although the existence of LOC can have some bearing on the likelihood of making a full recovery, it is not necessary for a person to become unconscious before that person may suffer a TBI. Physicians with expertise in TBI like to focus on "alteration of consciousness" as opposed to LOC. Any alteration in mental state, like confusion or disorientation, following a trauma is one indication of a TBI.

Although LOC is unnecessary to support a diagnosis of TBI, its absence may pose challenges in the legal claim. This is particularly true if the TBI victim complains of significant TBI symptoms or deficits and/or if the head trauma is minor. In these cases my experience has been that the insurance company will mount a very aggressive defense by arguing that the TBI victim's problems are due to other pre-existing factors or that the person is a malingerer. The insurance company attorneys and their experts will do everything they can to appeal to the jurors' suspicions that the TBI victim is exaggerating for the purpose of secondary gain (i.e., to secure a high settlement or verdict).

How to Recognize TBI Symptoms in Your Child

The Brain Injury Association calls TBI the "silent epidemic," because many children have no observable impairments following a head injury. If you talk to a neurologist who specializes in treating TBI survivors, he or she will also tell you that the condition of TBI often goes undiagnosed in the medical community. Many times TBI symptoms can be masked by other physical injuries that may cause chronic pain, depression, or emotional distress and anxiety. The physician may focus on these more observable physical problems and chalk up TBI symptoms to the secondary effects of physical trauma. This is another reason why TBI may not be diagnosed until weeks, months, or even years following the initial trauma.

TBI symptoms can vary depending on the extent and location

of the head injury, and sometimes on the age or development of the child. But symptoms involving concentration problems, slower mental processing, inability to focus, memory and language difficulties, vision problems, and changes in social or personal behavior are quite serious. One or more of these symptoms may be temporary or long lasting. Oftentimes the symptoms will appear within days following the trauma, although there is disagreement in the medical community about how long it can take for TBI symptoms to first appear. But again, the TBI symptoms may be masked by other physical injuries and thus appear as though they first appeared long after the trauma.

In my practice I regularly see TBI cases involving children who display a complex array of problems following head trauma. These include:

1. *Physical impairments.* These include speech, vision, and hearing impairments, as well as light sensitivity, headaches, seizures, partial paralysis of one or both sides of the body, and balance problems.

2. *Cognitive impairments.* These include long- and short-term memory issues, impaired concentration, mental processing difficulties, and language problems.

3. *Psychosocial, behavioral, and emotional impairments.* These problems can manifest as fatigue, emotional outbursts, inability to control anger, depression, personality changes, impaired coping skills, and the feeling of being overwhelmed in response to normal daily activities.

Any or all of the above symptoms may occur in varying degrees and last for varying time periods. Sometimes one or more of these symptoms can become permanent and result in life-changing problems in the child's life and in the lives of the child's parents and family members. But the vast majority of children will recover from mild TBI symptoms within 1 to 12 months, according to various studies. Nonetheless, improvement and reduction of symptoms following TBI may take as long as two years.

Parents should watch their children closely over the course of several days following a head trauma to determine whether classic TBI symptoms exist and, if so, to what degree. A prompt consultation with a medical doctor is necessary if your child demonstrates extreme fatigue, ongoing headaches, disorientation, behavioral or emotional problems, or other significant symptoms that interfere with daily activities.

Proving Traumatic Brain Injury (TBI)

Since most brain injury cases in litigation involve mild TBI (MTBI), the existence of the condition is often a central and disputed issue in the case. Most of the time the MTBI victim's diagnostic imaging tests (i.e., X-ray, CT and MRI scans) will appear normal. This is because the damage to brain tissue, consisting of nerve fibers and cells, is often microscopic and therefore may not be detected by conventional imaging techniques.

The mechanism of injury in MTBI is often referred to as "Diffuse Axonal Injury" (DAI) because it involves the tearing and/or stretching of axons, which are the neural processes that allow one neuron to communicate with another. The abrupt or sudden acceleration and/or deceleration of the brain can cause a "shearing injury," which refers to the damage inflicted on the brain tissue as it slides over other tissue and results in tearing and/or stretching of axons.

In brain injury cases involving children, the vast majority experience some degree of DAI. This type of injury can also result in secondary chemical changes to the brain over the course of several days following the initial injury. These chemical changes can also damage axons, and this process is thought to be another source of the symptoms common to MTBI. Children may be especially vulnerable to DAI because in their early developmental stage they are more physically vulnerable to trauma. Thus, it is not unusual for a child who suffers MTBI to develop new cognitive problems several days after the initial injury.

In my experience, the vast majority of child MTBI cases

involving DAI will also involve an aggressive defense mounted by the negligent party's insurance carrier and its lawyers. They will try to take advantage of the lack of "objective proof" of the brain injury itself and rely heavily upon the normal x-ray and CT and MRI scans that may have been taken of the child. For this reason it is extremely important that the child be represented by competent counsel who has experience in child brain injury cases. The experienced attorney will usually have the requisite knowledge and skill to address and overcome the insurance company's army of lawyers and experts who seek to minimize or refute the existence of the child's brain injury.

Proving Impairment of Brain Function—The Neuropsychological Evaluation

Another critical component of the child TBI case involves proving and measuring the degree of impairment in brain function. When we discuss brain function we are talking about the ways we use our brain. Brain dysfunction following TBI is typically measured in the following areas: (1) executive function, (2) language skills, (3) verbal memory, (4) attention, (5) sensory/motor, (6) emotion, and (7) organizational efficiency. The field of neuropsychology encompasses the study of the relationship between brain function and behavior. It involves the application of this knowledge to the functional and behavioral investigation of brain-injured people. Neuropsychology is concerned with the behavioral expression of brain dysfunction, either as a result of trauma or an abnormality affecting the brain.

The neuropsychologist uses a battery of tests and interviews occurring over the course of a few hours in one day, or several hours over a few days, to help measure brain impairment or dysfunction. These tests are standardized and validated based on specific segments of the population (e.g., adults vs. children). The test results are then measured against the norm (the rest of the population) to help the neuropsychologist determine brain dysfunction in any one measurable area. In the case of children, the neuropsychologist should have experience evaluating child TBI victims. The testing and manner of testing will be different from that used for adults. The tests used by neuropsychologists on children can provide information on the child's ability to learn, communicate, plan, organize, and relate to other people. The neuropsychological assessment will provide critical information that parents and teachers can use to build effective educational plans for the brain-injured child.

Future Implications for Children with TBI

For many years most of the medical community believed that children with TBI had a much greater chance of recovery than did adults with TBI. The theory was that children's brains had still not fully developed at the time of the TBI, which allowed the brain to more easily adapt to and compensate for brain damage. New studies have shown that this belief is untrue. We now know that a child TBI victim can actually experience more problems several years after the trauma. For example, a child's frontal lobes develop relatively late in a child's growth, so damage to this area of the brain may not be evident until the child reaches adolescence. The frontal lobes control social interaction and interpersonal skills. If a young child's TBI damages the frontal lobes of the brain, there could be serious problems with that child's ability to relate to other people once the child enters into adulthood.

Similarly, the child may need to confront increasingly difficult challenges with older age, like having to devote more time and effort to study harder subjects in school. Yet the child's abilities to meet these challenges may have been permanently damaged at the time of injury. If the injury occurred years earlier, parents may be completely unaware of the connection between the TBI and the child's later social and learning difficulties. If these apparently new difficulties show up years after the head trauma, it may be necessary to have the child undergo a new assessment of the disability. Unfortunately, a final assessment of the child's TBI cannot take place in most lawsuits due to stringent time requirements imposed by the law. We have the ability to use evidence from medical treatment and expert assessments of the child occurring close in time (a few years) following the injury. When it is time to settle the case, the child's attorney and experts should be prepared to discuss with the insurance company the unknown future implications following TBI in children.

Prior Medical Conditions

The insurance company and its experts will almost always request access to the child's prior medical and school records to see if there are any medical or psychological conditions that pre-existed the TBI. Many times children who are the victims of TBI will be too young to have any significant prior medical conditions that may impact the assessment of the case. But I see a sizeable percentage of TBI children who do have a prior history of certain recognized conditions, such as Attention Deficit Disorder (ADD), Attention Deficit Hyperactivity Disorder (ADHD), and other psychological disorders or conditions. I have learned in my practice of representing TBI children that these pre-existing diagnoses may be wrong, or that they do not fully meet the diagnostic criteria as adopted by the medical and/or psychological community. Children who do have pre-existing psychological problems often manifest symptoms that are similar, if not identical, to TBI. Therefore, it is imperative that the TBI child's medical history is scrutinized in detail and that the appropriate medical and psychological experts are retained early on in the case to verify the condition and to apportion the symptoms to any pre-existing condition, if necessary.

Skilled experts involved in the case can also help determine whether any pre-existing emotional or behavior problems are situational as opposed to being caused by a recognized medical condition. For example, children of divorce can exhibit situational anxiety, depression, and other behaviors similar to TBI symptoms. The child's complete social and family history will often need to be sorted out from the post-TBI symptoms.

This effort can make a huge difference when trying to determine whether symptoms following the head trauma are actually due to the TBI or some other cause. Of course, having a credible expert in your corner to separate out any pre-existing medical, psychological, social, and/or economic factors may contribute to a successful outcome of the case.

Using Skilled, Competent, and Reputable Experts

In most TBI cases that involve a legal claim, it will be necessary to use an expert or multiple experts to prove the extent of injury and the need for past and future treatment, to separate or apportion any pre-existing conditions, and to support any claim of impairment and/or disability. Therefore, the selection of an appropriate expert is one of the most important factors that will influence the outcome of a TBI case. As an attorney who regularly handles TBI cases involving children, I look for experts who can integrate a number of clinical findings made by the child's healthcare providers into a clear picture of a child living with a brain injury. I want my experts to relate the clinical and diagnostic findings to the child's everyday life so that the jury or the insurance company gets a compelling picture of how the child's brain injury affects his or her life.

There are usually four types of experts used in TBI cases. These include medical experts, neuropsychological experts, vocational experts, and economic loss experts (including life-care planners and economists). Sometimes the academic and professional credentials of the expert may make a difference in the ability to successfully resolve the case. Other times the ability of the expert to teach and explain TBI, along with its devastating impact on the child and the child's family, can be an important qualification that may persuade the defense to settle the claim. The unique facts and circumstances of the case may dictate which type of expert and the number of experts the attorney will retain. Because experts are a critical component in a successful TBI case, it is usually beneficial to retain competent counsel early on so there is sufficient time for the attorney to locate, hire, and brief each expert who may be necessary to support the merits of the case.

Gathering Evidence

Gathering the necessary information to support a TBI case is obviously very important in TBI litigation. Oftentimes the information may be lost or forgotten over time, because TBI cases can take months or even years to resolve. Therefore, it is critical to gather important information early on. This information may include witness statements, photographs, police reports, school records or teacher notes, and prior medical information. All too often parents come to an attorney long after their child sustained a TBI, and sometimes too late for the attorney to obtain certain evidence about the case that may have an impact on the outcome. My advice is to at least consult with a TBI lawyer early on following your child's injury so that information and evidence can be located and preserved.

Educational Implications

Although TBI is more common than people imagine, many school professionals and educators fail to realize that some learning problems may be associated with a traumatic brain injury. Oftentimes a child with TBI may be classified as learning disabled, or simply as a "slow learner." As a result, TBI children may not receive the full support and assistance they need.

When children with TBI return to school, their educational and emotional needs are different from what they were before the injury. Many children can remember how they functioned before the TBI injury, which may compound the child's level of frustration and feelings of hopelessness. This can lead to educational and social changes that will require professional help. Because of these difficulties, parents will want to plan the child's return to school very carefully. Meeting with teachers and other school professionals to consider special education resources is recommended. The school should thoroughly evaluate the child before the child's return to school.

Parents will also find it helpful to provide the school with copies of the child's medical records and expert reports, which will usually adequately describe, illustrate, and quantify the child's limitations and disabilities. An individual educational plan can then be developed for the child. Such a plan will help the child make a much smoother transition back into the classroom and provide the child with the necessary educational and emotional support.

Choosing Experienced Counsel

The selection of an attorney in child TBI cases is an extremely important decision. The TBI attorney will be responsible for investigating the facts, acquiring documentation to support the claim, developing legal theories, identifying and selecting appropriate experts, and performing all of the other tasks associated with litigation (e.g., drafting papers, taking depositions, handling pretrial preparation). Because many TBI cases can take years to resolve, parents will want to choose an experienced TBI attorney with whom they feel comfortable, and who has their child's best interests at heart.

Chapter Five

The Legal Process for Child Injury Claims

The legal process for child injury claims differs from the legal process for cases brought by adults. For starters, a child under the age of 18 is considered a minor. In Washington, a minor cannot file a lawsuit on his or her own. This can only be done by a *guardian* appointed by the court. A guardian is someone who the court believes will adequately protect the child's interests and do what is best for the child in the legal case that is being filed on the child's behalf.

To start a lawsuit, a *petition* must be filed, asking the court to appoint a suitable guardian who will bring the lawsuit on the child's behalf. Oftentimes the guardian appointed by the court will be the child's parent or parents. However, there may be a problem with using the child's parents to act as guardians. For example, if the child was injured in an automobile accident that was caused by the child's parent, then the child's claim against the parent creates a conflict of interest that will prohibit that parent from acting as the guardian in the lawsuit. But a conflict may still exist if the child merely has a potential claim against the parent. If there is any evidence suggesting that the defense might argue the parent was partially or wholly responsible for the child's injuries, it is usually a good idea to find another person to act as guardian on the child's behalf.

Once the court grants the petition, an order is entered, stating that the guardian is authorized to bring a lawsuit on behalf of the child. In addition to the petition, there are additional documents called *pleadings* that must be filed in court along with a fee paid to the clerk. These pleadings are called the *summons* and *complaint*. The summons informs the person being sued that a lawsuit is being filed and that a response to the lawsuit is due within a certain period of time. The complaint describes the legal basis for the allegations against the person being sued. The complaint will also set forth facts that support the cause of action. A complaint must be reasonably specific and inform the person being sued of the grounds supporting the claim.

The person who files a lawsuit is called the *plaintiff*. The person or entity that is being sued is called the *defendant*. Technically, the plaintiff is considered the guardian acting on behalf of the child. The plaintiff must arrange to personally serve a copy of the summons and complaint on the defendant. You only have a certain amount of time to settle your case or to file a lawsuit and then personally serve the defendant. In Washington, this time is usually 3 years from the date of the accident.[21] This deadline is called the *statute of limitations*. In claims involving minor children, the statute of limitations period is usually tolled (delayed) and will not start to run until the child's 18th birthday. Then the child has three years until the child's 21st birthday to settle the claim or file a lawsuit.

It is a dangerous practice to wait until the statute of limitations period is about to expire before settling a claim or filing a lawsuit. If a lawsuit is filed right before the deadline and if the defendant cannot be found, or if the wrong defendant is served, the case could be dismissed and the plaintiff gets nothing. For this reason, it may be prudent to hire an attorney well before the statute of limitations expires. Many attorneys will refuse to accept a case when the statute of limitations period is about to expire because there may be insufficient time to investigate the case, file suit, and locate and personally serve the proper defendant.

After the lawsuit is filed and the defendant is served, both sides participate in a process of asking for and exchanging information about the case. This process is called *discovery*. Each side is allowed to investigate what evidence and witnesses may

---

21. There are exceptions, of course, depending on the facts of the case. That is why an experienced attorney should be consulted if there are any questions about what time limit may apply to a particular case.

be introduced at trial. The discovery process may entail sending or answering written questions (called *interrogatories*) and requests for production documents and other tangible materials that are relevant to the case. In cases involving minor children, the defendant's attorney will be allowed to access the child's medical and school records.

The discovery process may also include a *deposition*. A deposition is a face-to-face meeting where the attorneys are allowed to ask a witness questions under oath while a court reporter transcribes the session. Any witness who may offer testimony at trial can be deposed, including the plaintiff, the plaintiff's doctors, and the plaintiff's friends and family. In cases involving the deposition of a child, certain conditions may be requested by the attorney and ordered by the court. The purpose of these conditions may be to implement certain safeguards and limitations for the protection of the child, like how long the deposition will last, what subjects may be inquired into, and where the deposition will take place. The attorney should speak to the child and the child's parents and guardian about what to expect at the deposition. The guardian and/or parents will usually want to attend the deposition as well. The deposition is an important legal proceeding that should involve preparation on the part of the attorney and the person or child who is going to be deposed.

The discovery phase may also include a request by the other side that the child submit to a medical examination, or a psychological or neuropsychological evaluation, or all three. When a lawsuit involves a claim for personal and psychological injuries, the law permits the defendant to use a doctor or psychologist chosen by the defense to examine and evaluate the injured person. This can be a stressful event, particularly in cases involving children. The attorney representing the child will want to make sure there are certain safeguards and limitations in place before the examination goes forward. Oftentimes those conditions may be contested by the defendant's attorney and this will necessitate a judge to decide the matter. Sometimes these conditions may include having the examination videotaped, allowing a representative for the child to attend the exam, as well as other conditions to ensure that the exam is fair and does not unduly burden or distress the child. For instance, in my office we have a fairly specific stipulation, which must be signed by the defense attorney, that imposes several conditions and restrictions on how the examination may proceed.

Depending on which county the lawsuit is filed in, the discovery phase can take many months or sometimes more than a year. When discovery is completed, and each side knows what evidence will be offered at trial, the parties may then begin to conduct settlement discussions. Sometimes the parties will engage in alternative ways to resolve the case, such as mediation. In mediation, the parties agree to hire a retired judge or an experienced attorney who will assist the parties in reaching a settlement. Mediation is voluntary and nonbinding (unless a settlement is reached). A mediation session is also confidential, so anything that is said during the session cannot be used at trial. Many times mediation can be used to successfully resolve a case involving children. Mediation sessions can be held over the course of one day or over several days, depending on the complexity of the case.

The settlement of a child's injury case also requires court approval. A *Settlement Guardian ad Litem* (SGAL) must also be appointed by the court (please refer to chapter seven, which explains the settlement process for child injury claims). It may be advantageous to appoint the SGAL early in the case so that this person can be fully apprised of all developments during the course of the litigation. Sometimes it may be advantageous to have the SGAL attend and/or participate in mediation to assist the attorney in settlement talks.

If the case does not settle after discovery has ended, the case will proceed to trial. Each side has the option of trying the case before a judge or jury. A jury trial does not happen automatically. One party must specifically request that the case be decided by a jury as opposed to a judge. Most often the defense will request a jury. This is accomplished by filing a document in court called a *jury demand* and then paying a *jury fee* to the clerk. Court rules usually require that certain documents must be filed and exchanged within 30 to 60 days before the trial date. These documents may include witness and exhibit lists, motions, trial memorandums, and jury instructions, among others.

Understandably, most parents want to avoid going to trial in their child's personal injury case. Trials are stressful and can cause additional anxiety for everyone involved. Usually a trial is the last resort to resolve the child's case. Oftentimes the insurance company will not want a serious or significant child injury case to go to trial, particularly when there is no serious dispute about fault for the accident and the severity of the injury. However, some insurance companies have a reputation for utilizing "scorched earth" litigation tactics, needlessly forcing and prolonging the litigation process in an effort to wear down the child's attorney and force a smaller settlement. Sometimes this will include forcing an unnecessary trial, particularly if the insurance company is convinced that the child's attorney has little experience in trying accident cases in court.

Usually, it is only by threatening and preparing for trial that the child's attorney will be able to secure a reasonable and just settlement offer for the child. This is why it is extremely important that the parent retain an attorney who has experience trying cases in court. You don't want to hire a lawyer for a serious injury case only to find out a few weeks or months before trial that the lawyer has either never tried a case in court or that the lawyer is afraid to try the case. In those situations, it may be too late to hire another attorney to take over. Many of the most experienced and reputable personal injury attorneys who handle child injury cases refuse to take over a case so late in the process, especially if the trial date is only a few months away. Of course, there may be exceptions, but this is usually a situation for parents to avoid.

A trial will also necessitate a decision about whether the injured child should appear and/or testify in court. Not every case requires the testimony of the injured child. There are strategic reasons for and against having the child testify in court. The primary consideration has to be the health and best interests of the child. If testimony in court will cause too much stress and anxiety, an alternative is to videotape the child's testimony outside of court and then show the video to the jury. Each case is different, and the decision will rest on the specific facts of a case and the attorney's judgment on the best course of action.

Chapter Six

The Wrongful Death of a Child

Nothing is perhaps more tragic or sad than the wrongful death of a child. As a parent myself, I cannot imagine anything more painful than losing one of my own children. I can only guess how painful this loss must be for a parent. The pain of the loss may be magnified even more because of the manner in which the child died-for example, if the child's death was due to another person's negligence.

Because this book covers the subject of child injury claims, it would be incomplete without addressing the subject of a child's wrongful death caused by another's negligent or reckless conduct. There are special laws in place that address this type of claim. On the one hand, the thought of a parent asking for compensation for the loss of a child may seem offensive or even repulsive to some. Clearly, no amount of money will ever bring back the child or make up for such a terrible loss. On the other hand, the law recognizes such a claim and gives a parent a specific right of redress against the responsible party. The recovery of compensation may play a part in holding the responsible party accountable for such a terrible harm, and may also act as a deterrent to future similar acts. The claim may also assist parents in the grieving process and help bring closure, although the memory of that event will almost certainly never go away. There is no doubt that a parent who loses a child will always grieve for that child until the day that parent dies.

For those parents who are experiencing such a tragic loss, I want this chapter to make them aware of the specific laws, procedures, and issues that may arise in a wrongful death case brought for the death of their child. In Washington, a wrongful death claim is governed by certain laws called *statutes*. Unlike a personal injury claim, the wrongful death claim may be authorized only by the legislature. A wrongful death claim is based on statutory law-as opposed to common law, which are laws created by our courts in other past cases. The laws governing such a claim may differ from state to state. Usually, but not always, the law of the state where the death occurred will be the law that controls the cause of action against the responsible party.

Washington's Wrongful Death Law

The state of Washington permits a parent to recover damages for the loss of a minor child, as long as the parent has regularly contributed to the support of the child.[22] The requirement that a parent must regularly contribute to the support of the child was a recent change to the law. This change was made to prevent a parent (often a father) who never or rarely supported the child during the child's lifetime from thereafter profiting financially from the child's death. The question of whether the parent regularly contributed to the support of the child is a question of fact. This means that it is up to the judge or jury[23] to determine whether the parent regularly supported the child according to the facts of the case.

In the context of the specific wrongful death statute, the term "support" generally means providing for a child's needs for housing, food, clothing, education, and healthcare. Usually, a noncustodial father who is obligated by a court order to make child support payments can meet this requirement by showing compliance with the order.[24] Presumably, a parent who pays

---

22. RCW 4.24.010.
23. Remember, if no jury demand has been filed in the court,,the case will be decided by the judge. See chapter five: The Legal Process for Child Injury Claims.
24. See *Guard v. Jackson*, 83 Wn. App. 325, 921 P.2d 544 (1996), *aff'd*, 132 Wn.2d 660, 940 P.2d 642 (1997).

child support every month is one who regularly contributes to the support of a child.

But what if a parent misses several months of support, or the parent owes several thousands of dollars in back support? What if the parent pays for some types of support (like food and housing), but not others (like insurance and private school)? Did the parent regularly support the child in those situations? Those questions are not easily answered. The judge or jury would have to determine whether a parent who owes back child support can also "regularly" contribute to the support of the child for purposes of recovering damages in an action for the wrongful death of that child.

Washington's wrongful death law creates only one cause of action, meaning that only one lawsuit may be commenced against the party responsible for the child's death. But if the child's parents are not married, or are separated, damages may be awarded to each parent separately as the jury or judge finds just and equitable. If one parent brings the wrongful death lawsuit and the other parent is not named in the lawsuit, the unnamed parent is entitled to receive notice of the suit, including a copy of the complaint that is filed in court. Notice must be accomplished by personal service. This requirement of notifying the other parent only applies if that parent's paternity has been established, which is usually accomplished by a court or administrative order.

The notice to the other parent must state that this parent must join as a party to the suit within twenty days or the right to recover damages under this section shall be barred. The failure of the other parent to appear in the lawsuit in a timely fashion shall bar that parent's right to recover any part of an award made to the other parent who instituted the lawsuit. There may be exceptions, such as when one parent is out of the country or in the military. Unfortunately, the language of the statute does not address these types of situations. In any event, the parent who has been properly notified of the lawsuit should act promptly and consult with experienced legal counsel.

Wrongful Death of a Fetus

Washington's wrongful death statute will also apply to an unborn fetus as long as the fetus was "viable." Usually, a viable fetus is one that was healthy and was expected to be born healthy had the death of the fetus not occurred. The wrongful death of that fetus is a recognized cause of action under the statute. What this means is that a child does not have to be physically born before a claim for wrongful death may go forward.

Legal Process for Wrongful Death Claim

The legal process for a wrongful death case is similar to other types of injury cases, except that the only person who may legally bring a claim is the *Personal Representative* (PR) of the child's estate. The PR must be appointed by the court. A petition is filed that asks the court to appoint a person as the PR. In the case of the wrongful death of a child, the PR is often a parent (unless, of course, a conflict exists). The PR will then have full authority to prosecute the action, including accepting settlement offers with the consent of the Settlement Guardian ad Litem.

If someone other than the PR files the wrongful death lawsuit, the court will dismiss the action if requested by the defendant. Therefore, it is important that the parents consult with an experienced attorney to properly file the petition and obtain the order appointing a PR before the wrongful death action is filed.

Damages for Wrongful Death of a Child

The damages recoverable for the wrongful death of a child include medical, hospital, and medication expense, and the loss of *consortium* (love, companionship, services, and support) that the child provided to the parents. The parents are also entitled to recover damages for the loss of financial support that the parents received from the child, up to the time when the child reaches the age of majority. To recover lost financial support, the parents usually have to show a history of receiving support from the child before that child's death.

The parents may also recover damages for the loss of love and companionship of the child and for injury to or destruction of the parent-child relationship. The actual amount recoverable will depend on the facts of each individual case, but will often depend on various factors like the age, health, and capacity of the child and the situation of the surviving parents.

Damages for the loss of love and companionship of the child and for injury to or destruction of the parent-child relationship may also encompass recovery for the parents' own grief, mental anguish, or suffering caused by the death of their child. These damages may also be reflected in each parent's need for individual expenses necessarily caused by the child's death, like the expense of reasonable and necessary psychological treatment, counseling, and medication. Oftentimes it will be prudent to present expert psychiatric or psychological testimony to support the parent's claim for these damages.

Damages may also be recovered for the parents' loss of companionship, including the loss of mutual society and protection of the deceased child, in an amount that is fair and equitable under the circumstances.

Wrongful Death of Adult Child

The specific statute that permits an action for the wrongful death of a child applies only to minor children (under the age of 18). If the child is 18 years or older, a different statute applies. In the case of the wrongful death of an adult, Washington has created two tiers of beneficiaries who may recover damages. In the first tier, the wrongful death action is brought for the benefit of a surviving spouse and/or children. In the second tier, the action is brought on behalf of a surviving parent or sibling who may be dependent on the deceased for support.[25] Thus, a parent

---

25. See RCW 4.20.020.

can only recover for the wrongful death of an adult child if that parent was dependent on that child for support.

The phrase "dependent for support" is interpreted by the courts to mean financial dependence. A parent of an adult child must be financially dependent on the child at the time of the child's death as a condition for recovering damages for the wrongful death of that adult child. The statute also requires the parent to be a resident of the United States at the time of the adult child's death.

Take, for example, the case of an adult male who dies in a traffic accident caused by another person. The man is married and has two children. In that situation, the man's surviving wife and children can maintain a cause of action for wrongful death against the other driver. If that man is unmarried with no children, the man's surviving parents may bring a wrongful death action but only if the parents can show they were financially dependent on their son at the time of his death. This requirement is part of a law that was first enacted more than one hundred years ago, when it was much more common for adult children to financially support their parents. Today most parents are financially independent and do not need to rely on the financial assistance of their children. As a result, the law as it stands now can cause some unjust results.

Let's look at another example: the case of a child whose wrongful death is caused shortly after the child's 18th birthday. In that situation, the parents have no legal means to recover against the responsible party unless the parents can show that they were financially dependent on their young child-a situation that almost never occurs. The law needs to be changed to reflect the current norms of society involving the relationship of parents with their adult children. A parent does not have to be financially dependent on an adult child for the death of that child to cause a significant amount of pain and loss for that parent regardless of the financial consequences of death. For this reason the law should be changed to remove the financial dependence condition.

52

Choosing Experienced Counsel

The selection of an attorney in a wrongful death case involving a minor child is very important. The attorney should have experience in wrongful death cases, whether settling or litigating these cases to verdict. One challenging aspect of a case involving the wrongful death of a child is proving the amount of damages that the parents and the estate may be entitled to receive. As stated earlier, the calculation of damages may be problematic because the child's death occurred at a young age and therefore it may be difficult to calculate future lost earnings and the intangible losses sustained by the parents. An experienced and skilled attorney can find creative and compelling ways to establish the losses so the insurance company or a jury will agree to pay reasonable compensation that is commensurate with those losses.

In my practice, we also use focus groups to help us evaluate wrongful death cases. A focus group is a group of individuals who review evidence and listen to testimony and arguments about the case from both sides. These individuals are often picked from voter registration records or other public documents. The idea is to select people whom the attorney may also find in a jury pool so that a fair evaluation of the case can be accomplished. A focus group can assist in determining the range of value of a case, and give the attorney creative ideas of how to present the case to a jury in trial. Of course, a focus group will never mimic or simulate a real trial, so caution should be exercised. Results can be skewed if you present the case in such a way that the evidence or arguments are slanted to one side. In any event, a properly conducted focus group can assist the parties in preparing the attorney for settlement talks or trial and in determining the value of a child injury case.

Chapter Seven

Legal Issues Involving Children and Dog Bites

One of the most common types of child injury claims that I see in my practice (second only to auto accidents) involves dog bites. In chapter one I cite some statistics from reputable sources, which confirm that dog bite attacks on children are more common than most people may think. These same studies also state that dog bite incidents are among the top five reasons why children are forced to visit hospital emergency rooms. Parents are thus well advised to keep close supervision of their children while a dog is present, especially if the dog is unknown or if the child has had little, if any, contact with the dog in question. In this chapter I will go over some of the legal issues involved in these types of cases.

Overview of Washington Dog Bite Statute

Historically, a person could only recover damages against a dog owner if it could be proven that the owner had prior knowledge of the dog's viciousness or propensity to bite. This law was called the "One Bite Rule" because it meant that every dog owner had one "free bite" before civil liability could be imposed. Fortunately, the Washington legislature recognized how unjust the law was. It was very difficult for a dog bite victim to prove that the owner had the requisite prior knowledge that the dog was dangerous. Proving what a dog owner knew about his dog before the injury occurred is extremely difficult, if not virtually impossible.

Several years ago Washington enacted a law (statute) that removed the requirement of proving the dog owner's prior knowledge. The law now holds that dog owners are strictly liable for any injuries or bites the dog inflicts on others, including children.[26] This means the owner is liable for a dog bite injury even if the dog has never bitten another human being and even if the dog has never previously acted in an aggressive manner. But there is one requirement: the injury must occur while the victim is in a public place or while lawfully present on private property. If the injury occurs on the property of the dog owner, the law requires that the victim must have been present on this property with the owner's consent or permission.

The law further states that a person must be lawfully on the dog owner's private property with the owner's *express* or *implied* consent. Express consent means that the dog owner specifically invited you onto his property. Implied consent means that the dog owner allowed you onto his property without specifically inviting you. For instance, the person who delivers the mail or makes a parcel delivery is one who is said to have been implicitly allowed by the landowner to enter onto the private property to complete the delivery. In the case of a child, the boy who regularly cuts a neighbor's lawn can be seen as one who is lawfully on private property with the owner's implied consent. Whether or not implied consent exists will obviously depend on the facts of the case.

In most dog bite cases I see involving children, there is no dispute that the child was either in a public place or lawfully on the dog owner's private property when the incident occurred. However, occasionally I am contacted by the parents of a child who was attacked by a dog while that child was trespassing on the dog owner's property. In those situations, the child will not have a successful claim under Washington's dog bite statute,

---

26. See RCW 16.08.040, which states, "The owner of any dog which shall bite any person while such person is in or on a public place or lawfully in or on a private place including the property of the owner of such dog, shall be liable for such damages as may be suffered by the person bitten, regardless of the former viciousness of such dog or the owner's knowledge of such viciousness."

which imposes strict liability. However, the child may still have a recognized cause of action under the common law, which I will explain in more detail later in this chapter.

Even if the child is bitten by a dog while in a public place or while lawfully on private property, liability may not attach if the dog was provoked. Washington law states that the provocation of the animal is a complete defense to a claim against the dog owner.[27] Whether provocation occurred will depend on the individual facts involved. But if the dog is intentionally hit, teased, or taunted and, as a result, bites the perpetrator, usually a claim for damages against the owner will not succeed. That defense seems reasonable since it would be unfair to allow someone to profit from a dog bite injury that was only caused by the intentional provocation of the animal in the first place.

But what about a very young child who is injured after that child unintentionally provokes the dog? Remember, a child under the age of 6 is presumed to lack the requisite knowledge and intent to engage in negligent behavior.[28] Thus, one may argue convincingly that a child under this age cannot legally provoke an animal, because the child has a limited capacity to understand what provocation means. On the other hand, a child older than 6 years is likely to be mature enough to understand that a dog should not be provoked. If there are facts to support a provocation defense, you can bet the insurance company and its lawyers will certainly argue this defense to avoid paying out any compensation.

Common Law Liability for Dog Bites

A dog bite victim may also pursue a claim for damages against the dog owner under common law theories of liability. The common law refers to those laws that are made by Washington courts over the years. These laws are found in the court opinions issued by the appellate courts, including the

27. See RCW 16.08.060.
28. Please see chapter two.

Washington State Supreme Court. A common law claim against a dog owner may be pursued *in addition* to a claim brought under the specific dog bite statute found at RCW 16.08.040. The two types of claims are not mutually exclusive.

Under Washington common law, a person who keeps or harbors a dog, and who knows or should reasonably know that the dog has vicious or dangerous propensities likely to cause the injuries complained of, is strictly liable for the injuries caused by the dog regardless of negligence committed by either the keeper of the dog or the injured person.[29] Any injury caused by such an animal subjects the owner to strict liability without the need to prove that the dog owner was negligent. Thus, a dog owner may be held liable for an injury if it can be proven that the owner had some prior knowledge of the dog's dangerous tendencies.

Under Washington common law, it is not necessary for a dog to have previously bitten someone for its owner to be presumed to have knowledge that it was likely to do so.[30] The only requirement is that the dog owner had some knowledge of a trait or propensity of the animal likely to cause the accident or injury complained of.[31] For example, if the owner previously knew that the dog liked to growl and snarl, or bare its teeth at young children, such knowledge may be enough evidence to hold the owner liable for injuries if the dog later attacks and bites a child.

Washington common law also permits an action against the owner of a dog based on a theory of negligence. Thus, if you can show that the dog bite was caused by the owner's failure to exercise ordinary care in some way, then liability may also attach. If the owner failed to restrain or care for the dog in a particular manner and this omission was a proximate cause of the injury inflicted by the dog, the owner could be liable for the harm. For example, if the owner knew that the dog liked to jump on people and then failed to exercise ordinary care to prevent this from happening, the owner may be responsible for any injuries

29. See *Brewer v. Furtwangler*, 171 Wash. 617, 18 P.2d 837 (1933).
30. *Mailhot v. Crowe*, 99 Wash. 623, 170 P. 131 (1918).
31. *Johnston v. Ohls*, 76 Wn.2d 398, 457 P.2d 194 (1969).

inflicted by the dog if it engaged in that behavior.

Let's revisit the example I wrote about earlier in the chapter involving a child who was attacked by a dog while trespassing on the owner's property. That child will likely not have a successful claim under the dog bite statute. But a common law claim against the dog owner could be successful if certain facts were present. If you could show that the owner knew that children regularly trespassed on the dog owner's property and that the owner knew that his dog had previously attacked other people under similar circumstances, one could make a compelling argument that the owner therefore had a duty to take additional precautions to prevent another attack by the dog. The cases that are brought under common law theories of liability rely heavily on the specific facts involved. In fact, attorneys like to call these cases "fact-specific" because the likelihood of success is almost entirely based on what version of the facts will be believed by the jury.

Who is the "Owner" of the Dog?

Occasionally a dispute arises about who actually "owns" the dog. For instance, if the person who harbors and takes care of the dog is not the true legal owner of the animal, can this person still be liable for the injuries inflicted by the dog? The answer is usually yes. Although the dog bite statute refers to liability of the dog "owner," there are court decisions that broadly define the owner to include one who possesses and/or cares for the dog.[32]

Furthermore, there may be various local regulations and ordinances that also broadly define who a dog owner is. For example, in King County a dog owner is broadly defined as "any person having an interest in or right of possession to the animal, or any person having control, custody, or possession of an animal...or by reason of the animal being seen residing consistently at a location, to an extent such that the person could be presumed to be the owner."[33] This definition is broad enough

---

32. See *Beeler v. Hickman*, 50 Wn. App. 746, 750 P.2d 1282 (1988).
33. See King County Code 11.04.020(P).

to include any person who harbors or keeps the dog for a period of time that is sufficient to cause one to believe that the person may be the true or legal owner even if that person is not.

Contributory Negligence and Assumption of Risk

The concepts of contributory negligence and assumption of risk may also apply in cases involving child dog bite injuries. The dog owner may be permitted to argue that the child was comparatively negligent for causing the injury. The defense of assumption of risk may also apply if the owner can prove that the child had knowledge of the dog's traits or propensities and that the injury was caused in whole or in part when the child assumed the risk of the particular facts giving rise to the child's injury. But these defenses may not be available if the child was under the age of 6 and thus legally incapable of engaging in negligent conduct or incapable of appreciating or assuming known risks associated with the dog in question.

Landlord Liability for Dog Bite

Occasionally I come across a case in which the incident occurred on property that was being leased to or rented by the dog owner. The question is therefore, can the landlord be held responsible for the dog bite injury even though the landlord doesn't own or harbor the dog? The answer is usually no. The Washington Supreme Court has held that a landlord cannot be held liable for the harm caused by a tenant's dog, even if the landlord had knowledge of the dog's vicious or dangerous propensities.[34]

---

34. See *Frobig v. Gordon*, 124 Wn.2d 732, 881 P.2d 226 (1994).

The Dog's Breed—Does It Matter?

This is a controversial issue. Some people believe strongly that certain breeds have innate traits of aggression that make them more likely to inflict harm on human beings than other types of breeds. Opponents of this view state that a dog's propensity for aggressive behavior is dictated primarily by the dog's owner or handler and by the manner in which that dog was trained and cared for early in its life.

On the one hand, certain breeds do appear to have a higher incident rate of inflicting harm on people, including children. According to Merritt Clifton, editor of the newspaper publication *Animal People*, the breeds of pit bull terriers, rottweilers, Presa Canarios, and their mixes accounted for 74 percent of reported attacks from 1982 through 2005. Sixty-eight percent of those attacks involved children. Following these breeds, the next group representing the highest occurrence of attacks included German shepherds, chows, and Akitas. But the question remains whether these breeds were responsible because of some innate characteristic associated with their breed or because they were more likely to be groomed and trained by their owners to act in an aggressive manner.

A hot topic these days is the issue of breed-specific legislation, sometimes called "breed ban laws." Some cities in various states have enacted specific legislation against certain breeds. They include cities in the states of California, Colorado, and Ohio. In Washington, the city of Yakima has adopted an ordinance that completely bans the ownership of pit bulls and their mixes, wolf-hybrids, and others. I am also aware that the city of Seattle has informally considered the issue, but the city council has so far refused to formally address the topic due to the lack of consensus among experts and/or council members. If we, as a community, continue to see more and more incidents of attacks committed by one or more of the more notorious breeds, it is likely that more cities or even the state legislature will enact laws that are breed-specific. The next question will be whether these laws will have any appreciable effect on reducing dog-bite incidents among specific breeds.

Concerns About Insurance

A primary concern in dog bite cases is whether there is adequate insurance to pay for the child's damages. Most homeowner insurance policies will provide coverage for injuries inflicted by the family dog. But each policy is different and should be reviewed carefully. If there is no insurance, it is extremely unlikely that the child will be able to receive compensation for damages. Yes, the dog owner can still be taken to court. But without a guaranteed source of recovery, most attorneys will refuse to incur the thousands of dollars of expense and spend the hundreds of hours necessary to take the case to trial.

Chapter Eight

The Settlement Process for a Child's Injury Claim

In Washington, there are special conditions that must be met in the settlement of a child injury claim. In every settlement of a minor's claim, whether filed in court or not, the Superior Court shall determine the adequacy of the proposed settlement and decide whether to reject or approve it.[35] To assist the court in determining whether a minor child settlement is reasonable, the court will also appoint a Settlement Guardian ad Litem (SGAL). Usually, the SGAL is an experienced attorney. The SGAL has the job of investigating the facts of the case, reviewing records and pleadings, interviewing the parents or legal guardians, and then determining whether the amount of the settlement is reasonable.

After the SGAL concludes the investigation, he or she must make a recommendation to the court on whether the settlement should be approved or rejected. A court hearing is then scheduled so the judge can formally decide whether the settlement is approved. Usually the child's attorney, the SGAL, and parents (and sometimes the child) must appear at the hearing to answer the judge's questions or concerns. The court will often rely heavily on the SGAL's recommendation about whether to reject or approve the settlement. Sometimes more than one hearing is necessary if the case is complex or if there are unusual issues that must be worked out.

There are costs associated with the court approval process.

---

35. See SPR 98.16W.

The SGAL has to be paid for his or her time. Filing fees or other incident costs may be incurred. Usually the negligent party's insurance carrier will agree to pay for these costs and fees. Sometimes the judge or commissioner who decides whether the settlement should be approved may also order that an insurance company must pay for the costs. The child's attorney usually does not get paid extra for the additional work involved in the court approval process. The attorney's fee is usually paid from the settlement recovered on behalf of the child.

Role of Settlement Guardian ad Litem (SGAL)

A petition must be filed in court, formally asking the judge or commissioner to appoint the person who will act as the SGAL. That person must be approved by the court. There are certain educational and experiential prerequisites that a person must meet before he or she can be an approved SGAL. Usually, but not always, the SGAL is a licensed attorney. Sometimes people who occupy roles involving child advocacy (e.g., counselors, psychologists) can serve as court-approved SGALs.

Essentially the role of the SGAL is to investigate the relevant facts concerning the child's case and the proposed settlement. The SGAL analyzes the course(s) of action available to the child in the underlying action. The SGAL identifies the course(s) of action that the SGAL thinks will best serve the child's interests, and makes a report and recommendation to the court concerning those interests. The role of other parties involved, who often include the child's attorney and parents or guardian, is to assist the SGAL by providing information, answering questions, and highlighting any concerns. The SGAL's role is very important because the court cannot conduct its own investigation without exceeding its proper judicial function. Thus, in most cases the court will place a great deal of weight on the SGAL's investigation and recommendations.

The SGAL must conduct an investigation and compile a report containing his or her recommendation on whether the settlement should be approved or rejected. The SGAL's investigation usually includes reviewing all of the medical records, expert reports, pleadings, and other documentation to support the claim. The SGAL usually will want to talk to the child and/or the child's parents or guardian about the effect of the child's injuries and the settlement proposal. The SGAL will also want to talk to the child's attorney to understand all of the legal issues involved and the attorney's rationale for recommending that the settlement offer be approved.

The SGAL's report to the court is fairly detailed and specific. There are certain issues and questions that the report must address and/or explain. These issues or areas may include without limitation: (1) the SGAL's background and qualifications, (2) a description of the investigation conducted and names of people contacted, (3) a description of the incident giving rise to the claim and all defenses asserted by the other side, (4) a description of the child's injuries, treatment, and damages incurred, (5) a discussion of all possible sources of recovery and questions regarding insurance, (6) a description and recommendation of all liens and how they will be paid or resolved, (7) whether the fees and costs being claimed are reasonable, and (8) how the net proceeds will be disbursed and/or used on behalf of the minor child.

One of the issues for the SGAL to investigate and report on to the court is what to do about the child's net settlement proceeds (i.e., the amount of money left over after fees, costs, and liens have been paid). Basically, there are three options: (1) establishing a blocked bank account for the minor, (2) purchasing an annuity that will make future payments to the minor after he or she turns 18, or (3) creating a managed trust account for the benefit of the minor child. Sometimes a combination of the three options is utilized, depending on the amount of the settlement and the age of the child.

Blocked Account for Minor

One option is to place the settlement funds in a blocked account with a major bank. These funds may not be accessed by the child until the child turns 18 years of age. The account may only be accessed sooner with a court order. Usually the judge will not allow the child or the child's parents to access the funds before the child's 18th birthday unless there is a good reason, such as to pay for the child's ongoing medical treatment or educational needs. Oftentimes a blocked account is recommended where the net settlement proceeds are relatively small, i.e., under $25,000. Because the rate of return in a blocked account may be somewhat small, the funds in a blocked account can be used to purchase a renewable certificate of deposit that will offer the best rate of return.

Annuity Purchase

Another option is to use the settlement proceeds to purchase an annuity on behalf of the child. An annuity will provide a stream of payments to the child at different time intervals after the child turns 18 years old. These future payments are considered tax-free. Usually an annuity is recommended for larger sums of money because the rate of return is much better than that of a standard bank account or certificate of deposit. One down side of an annuity is that the child cannot under any circumstances access the settlement funds before the periodic payments begin. So if the child may have certain financial needs (e.g., ongoing medical care), it may be a better idea to put some of the funds into a blocked account so there is the ability to access these funds before the child's 18th birthday (albeit with a court order).

One advantage of purchasing an annuity is that one has enormous flexibility in determining the future periodic payment and the time interval of payments. For instance, future payments can be made on an annual basis lasting several years, or on a biannual, or quarterly basis. A lump sum balloon payment can be structured after providing for upfront smaller payments after the child's 18th birthday. Usually the court will not approve a structured payout that lasts too far in the future. This is because the child may be too tempted to sell all or part of the annuity at a significant discount. There are companies that exist to purchase annuities at a discount so people do not have to wait to receive their money. If an annuity purchase is an option that is being considered, the SGAL will usually discuss the pros and cons with the child's parents and jointly decide on a future annuity payment schedule that best fits the anticipated future needs of the child (i.e., to pay for college or vocational school).

Managed Trust Account

A final option is to use the settlement proceeds to establish a trust account. A trustee is appointed by the court to manage the account. The trustee cannot be a parent of the child or a family member. The trustee cannot have a residual beneficial interest in the trust proceeds. The trustee must be bonded or insured. Often the trustee is a professional trustee or a company that may act as trustee for many other trust accounts. The trustee is required to prepare an annual statement of income, expenses, current assets, and fees charged, and provide this statement to the guardian of the child (i.e., the beneficiary). The statement must be approved by the court. Because a trustee is also entitled to charge a fee for managing the trust and providing an annual report, the settlement proceeds usually need to be large enough to warrant this expense.

Seeking Court Approval

Once the SGAL has concluded the investigation and issued a report, the child's attorney must draft and file a petition with the court asking the judge or court commissioner to approve the settlement. A hearing will be set. The child's attorney, the parents, and the SGAL will usually have to attend the hearing. Sometimes it is a good idea for the child to appear, depending on age and the issues involved. The hearing allows the court to ask any questions about the SGAL's investigation and report. Sometimes the court will ask the parents questions to learn more about the child's injuries or prognosis. If the court approves of the settlement, an order will be entered setting forth the basis for approval and ruling how the settlement proceeds will be disbursed and held and/or invested on behalf of the child.

With a final order approving the settlement, the child's attorney should make efforts to set up a blocked account with a financial institution (if that is where some of the proceeds will be deposited). In the case of an annuity purchase, the child's attorney is expected to furnish a copy of the order and other paperwork to the company who has sold and/or funded the annuity. In the case of a trust, the trustee should have been chosen and approved by the court so that the settlement proceeds can fund the trust. The child's attorney is required to draft and file written proof with the court verifying that the appropriate steps have been taken to comply with the court's ruling about where the settlement proceeds will go, and that the funds have been deposited into the blocked account or that the annuity has been purchased or that the trust has been established and funded.

It is important to understand that the settlement approval process concerning a minor child injury claim can take weeks or even several months, depending on the complexity of the case and the amount of proceeds involved. Sometimes the settlement process can be initiated early in the claim, enabling the SGAL to participate in settlement discussions with the other party's insurance carrier. Sometimes this may not be practical if there are other demands involved with the claim, like litigation or an impending trial date. Every case is different, and the parents should expect to speak to the attorney about what to expect in their child's claim.

Impact of Minor Settlement on Other Benefits or Government Assistance

Special care must be taken to determine whether the settlement will impact the child's right to receive any asset or income-sensitive benefits or certain governmental assistance under public benefit programs. A seriously disabled child could be eligible for local, state, and federal benefits based on the child's disability. These benefits are also called "collateral source benefits" and may include benefits under Medicare, Medicaid, Social Security Income (SSI), specialized education (20 USC § 1400 et seq.), housing (HUD and local housing authority), attendant care, and other programs. Yet to be eligible for most of these benefits, the claimant must not have access to available resources of more than $2,000 (with certain exceptions known as exempt resources). A child's settlement proceeds could be considered sufficient resources available to eliminate that child's eligibility for these programs.

Sometimes the SGAL will have some knowledge of the impact that the settlement may have on the child's eligibility for public entitlement programs. But many times an expert must be hired to determine whether the settlement should be structured in a way to preserve the child's right to recover future public benefits. There are ways to do this, such as setting up a Special Needs Trust (SNT). Due to intricacies in this area of the law, assets held in the SNT are not considered "available" to the claimant, so the claimant's eligibility for public programs is preserved. In any event, if there is any chance that the settlement may impact the child's ability to recover future benefits under any one of the various local, state, or federal public entitlement programs, an expert in disability benefits law should be retained.

I have heard of cases where the child's attorney failed to consider the impact of a settlement on a child's right to recover future government benefits. This can have devastating consequences because these benefits may provide the child with substantial and necessary financial assistance in the years to come. This is yet another important reason why parents should only hire an attorney who is experienced with the settlement process required in minor injury claims.

Chapter Nine

Determining the Value of a Child's Injury Claim

There is no magic formula or process by which someone can predict with certainty the amount of money that a child's injury case may be worth. About twenty-five to thirty years ago there was some limited consensus among lawyers and insurance adjustors that a claim might be worth three times the amount of medical expenses plus lost wages. But that so-called rule was really just a guideline for predicting how a jury might determine the value of any given case. Today no such guideline or consensus exists. There are so many different factors that may influence the value of a claim that it is virtually impossible to create some type of formula that can reliably predict the value of any given case.

Take, for example, a case where the injured person had undergone spine surgery and the total medical expenses came to $50,000. If the person had previous spine or back problems that pre-dated the accident, it is highly unlikely an insurance company would agree to settle the case for $150,000 or any other multiple of the medical expense. The same is true for injury claims involving children. One example is a child who sustains a mild traumatic brain injury in a car accident. If that same child exhibited ongoing TBI-like symptoms before the accident (e.g., emotional outbursts, inability to concentrate), the carrier will likely refuse to agree that all of the child's symptoms after the accident were in fact caused by that accident. In that type of case, the carrier may argue that only 50% or 75% of the treatment was related to the initial car accident injury. You get the idea. Each claim has to be evaluated based on the specific facts unique to that claim. So, although I wish a formula were used by insurance companies (it would make my job a lot easier!), that simply is not the case.

Injury cases involving children can be even more difficult when it comes to determining a value. This has to do with the child being young and physically immature. Estimates about the impact of an injury on future employment and relationships (e.g., marriage) can be highly speculative because the child has not yet attained the age when the results of the injury may be fully manifested. For this reason, trying to determine the future impact of a child's injury may be highly speculative and therefore difficult to calculate.

There is also a difference in the settlement value of a case versus the actual value a jury may decide. The settlement value of a case is always less than the actual value of a case. This is because the settlement value takes into account the enormous expense and risk of going to trial. The settlement value is always a judgment made by the parties. The settlement offer has to be high enough to persuade the claimant to accept the offer to avoid the increased risk and expense of going forward with litigation and a trial. If there is a strong defense concerning liability, that is, if the defense can show the likelihood of the jury finding that the defendant was not at fault for the accident, or that the plaintiff-child shares a good portion of the fault, then the settlement value of case will be reduced even further to reflect the risk that no or little fault may be assessed. Again, the merits of a particular defense should be thoroughly evaluated by competent and experienced counsel in order to make an appropriate risk-benefit analysis about going to trial.

Generally speaking, a case is worth the amount of damages inflicted on the person who has been injured. These damages may be easy to calculate, such as past and future medical charges, lost earnings, lost earning capacity, and property loss. But the law also states that the injured person has the right to recover compensation for other "intangible" harms. It is these "intangible" harms that are more difficult to calculate. Such harms may include those subjective harms that the child has experienced from the injury, including pain, agony, disability, loss of enjoyment, inconvenience, and mental anguish. The intangible harms are purely subjective, difficult to determine, and often vary among the people (or jurors) who are deciding the case. Ultimately, the value of a case is determined by the jury (or judge, if the case is tried to the court). After a case arises, the injured person's attorney and the at-fault person's insurance company (and the defense attorney, if the case is in litigation) are continually trying to evaluate how a jury might see the case and how much money a jury might award. Then each side will assign a value or a value range, and try to negotiate a settlement close to each side's own range.

An attorney will use his or her experience and expertise to help establish a reasonable range within which a jury might render a verdict. Nothing is certain, however. Any case can be lost at trial because juries are very unpredictable. You will never know what group of people you will get on a jury. Two different juries can produce two very different verdicts, even when presented with the same evidence and testimony. You may get a "good" group of jurors or a "bad" group. Common to popular myth, you cannot "select" a good jury over a bad one. Washington law only allows each side to strike 3 jurors out of a panel of 30 to 40 people. Thus, a trial is always to a certain extent a gamble. There is no guarantee that a jury will reach a favorable verdict, no matter how good you or the attorney believes the case is.

Sometimes it may take many months or years before the value of a case can be adequately assessed. One reason for this is the slow recovery or rehabilitation of the claimant. Another reason is the complexity of the injury or condition that may cause a significant delay in a firm diagnosis by the treating physician. Although many attorneys believe a case should not settle until the person obtains maximum medical improvement from the injury, it may not be prudent in the case of an injured child. Sometimes it takes many years before a child's condition becomes fixed and stable or fully known, but there may be a stronger need to recover compensation to help fund the child's treatment expense or other special needs. Sometimes the child's injuries can resolve or even disappear over many years (like a significant scar), so waiting to resolve the claim can actually mean a lower settlement value. The timeframe involved in settling a child's injury claim is really a judgment call by the child's parents, the attorney, and the SGAL.

There is another reason to start the litigation and/or settlement process sooner in the case of an injured child. The child's young age may also provide a compelling basis for the jury or insurance company to determine a higher level of compensation. Simply put, a young child can often evoke more sympathy and concern among jurors than an adult. A jury may be much more willing to award higher compensation if they see how vulnerable the child was at the time of injury. If the settlement of the claim is delayed until the child reaches young adulthood, this compelling advantage may be lost.

In most instances the value of a case is driven primarily by the extent and severity of the person's injuries. The particular facts giving rise to the claim of negligence against the other party may also have some influence. Other important factors to consider include the type, extent, and frequency of past medical treatment and the need for future treatment. Other factors that may affect the value of a case include, but are not limited to, the claimant's likeability and credibility, the extent and duration of the injuries, the claimant's age, whether the claimant missed time from work, the reputation or track record of the at-fault insurance company and the defense attorney, the specific legal or evidentiary issues involved in the case, the county or venue where the case has been or will be filed, and the dollar amount of settlements and verdicts for similar types of cases in the past.

No two cases are alike, even if the accident and/or injuries involved are nearly identical. The evaluation of two cases that appear to be similar on the surface may actually produce widely different evaluations due to the other factors listed above. Evaluating personal injury cases takes a lot of knowledge, experience, and some seasoned intuition. Without these traits you may be at a serious disadvantage when negotiating with the insurance adjustor. And unless you are in the business of evaluating and settling personal injury cases for a living, you should look to an experienced personal injury attorney for guidance.

Because of the increased difficulty of evaluating the damages in a child injury claim, it may be necessary to hire experts to help establish the extent of these damages. These experts may include vocational experts, life care planners, economists, psychologists, and/or psychiatrists. Oftentimes the skilled expert can help corroborate evidence and describe the effect that the injuries will have on the child many years in the future. This is even truer when the child was injured at a particularly young age.

There are other ways to help determine the value of a child injury case. For example, I routinely conduct focus group studies, sometimes called "mock trials," on my cases, including those involving injuries to children, to help me decide how much a case is worth.

The insurance company will evaluate the child's case by deciding the odds of winning against the range of a likely verdict. The company will decide on a settlement range that will always be less than the expected range of a jury's verdict. It is important to understand that the insurance company's settlement offer can never be introduced at trial. The jury will never know that an insurance company is in the picture, or the amount of the last offer received. These facts are routinely kept away from the jury according to our state's rules governing the admissibility of evidence. If a child's attorney makes a settlement demand that is too far over the insurance company's settlement range, negotiation is terminated. You cannot just ask for a huge amount of money and see what happens. Insurance companies rigorously track verdicts and settlements in similar types of cases. They also keep track of which attorneys will take cases to trial and how well they do.

In the end, the attorney must balance the risk of loss at trial or the risk of a jury verdict for less than the last settlement offer against the likelihood of a larger verdict being awarded. There is no formula for this analysis, and it can often be an uncertain "guesstimate."

Chapter Ten

Signing a Pre-injury Release Document on Behalf of a Child

A "pre-injury release" document is one that attempts to contractually limit or waive a party's right to pursue a claim against a third party for negligence. The document typically states that you agree not to sue or file a claim against another party if you are injured during a particular activity, even if that party negligently caused your injury. These documents are also called "exculpatory clauses," meaning that they seek to release a party from liability for negligent conduct that may occur in the future.

In Washington, a pre-injury release is generally enforceable but only in the setting of adult high-risk sports or recreational activities. Examples of these types of activities include snow skiing, mountain climbing, scuba diving, weight lifting, and other sports like basketball and football. The court will likely uphold the validity of the agreement as long as (1) the terms of the release are fairly clear, (2) the activity in question is considered high-risk, and (3) the alleged negligent conduct does not fall greatly below the standard of care for the protection of others.[36] The rationale for this view is that the activity presents certain known risks and the adult usually has a choice about whether to participate in the high-risk activity.

The question, however, is whether a pre-injury release can also be used to bar a child's potential claim for injury against a negligent third party. The answer is clearly, no. In 1992, the Washington Supreme Court ruled that a parent does not have

---

36. See *Wagenblast v. Odessa Sch. Dist. No. 105-157-166J*, 110 Wn.2d 845, 758 P.2d 968 (1988).

legal authority to waive a child's own future cause of action for personal injuries resulting from a third party's negligence. The case, *Scott v. Pacific West Mountain Resort*,[37] involved an action filed by parents and their child against a ski resort and ski school for injuries the child sustained in a skiing accident. Before the accident happened, the parents had signed an agreement containing an exculpatory clause that released the resort and the school from any future injuries or negligent behavior sustained by them or their child. Although the court upheld this agreement with respect to the parents, it refused to validate the agreement concerning the child's claims.

The basis for the *Scott* ruling was that the minor child was legally incapable of entering into such an agreement and that the parents did not have legal authority to release the child's future claims. Since a settlement of a child's claims cannot occur without court approval (see chapter seven), the court reasoned it did not make sense then to allow parents to contract away a child's future claim. In short, the court determined that the agreement was a violation of public policy and therefore was unenforceable with respect to the child's claim.

Although parents cannot legally enter into a pre-injury release on behalf of their child, this does not stop others from demanding that a pre-injury release be signed as a condition to letting the child participate in certain high-risk activities. Most of the third parties who request such an agreement are simply unaware that the law will not enforce it if the child should become injured due to that party's negligent conduct. However, just because a child is injured during a particular activity does not necessarily mean that the child will have a successful claim against another party.

Take, for example, the activity of sports. Children commonly get injured in sporting activities. Most of the time the child does not have a successful claim against the sponsor or organizer of the activity (e.g., school district, community organizer) because the injury is a recognized risk associated with that activity. The

---

37. *Scott v. Pacific W. Mountain Resort*, 119 Wn.2d 484, 834 P.2d 6 (1992).

phrase "assumption of risk" is one that is commonly used to describe the situation where a child participates in an activity subsequent to being aware of the risks of injury associated with that activity. Courts and juries in Washington are reluctant to allow a successful claim where the child's injury was one that was within the recognized and appreciable risks of harm associated with that activity, and not due to some other party's negligent conduct.

Here's an illustration. Usually, a child will not have a legal claim for injuries if that child suffers a broken bone while playing football. This activity is commonly recognized as one involving a high risk of harm. And a broken bone is simply one of those risks of harm that can occur when playing this sport. However, what if the broken bone was caused because the child was wearing defective equipment, the wrong equipment, or not enough equipment? Then a claim may lie against the manufacturer of the defective equipment, or against the coach or league that is responsible for issuing the equipment. For instance, a coach or league may be responsible if either one knowingly issued equipment that was too small, or if either one failed to issue sufficient equipment that is normally worn by a participant of the sport. In these types of cases, parents need to understand that the existence of a claim is very much dependent on the individual facts involved.

Chapter Eleven

Resources Available to Injured Children

Numerous resources are available to those children who have suffered injuries and disability. These resources exist at the local, state, and federal level. There may also be resources available through private insurance companies, depending on the type of insurance that exists and also on the circumstances giving rise to the child's injuries. This chapter is not intended to be exhaustive. Parents are advised to do their own research about the specific needs of their children. Nonetheless, this chapter should give you a good overview of some of the more common resources available to children who have sustained traumatic injuries.

Private Insurance

There is a difference between third-party insurance and first-party insurance. A third-party insurance company is the carrier for the at-fault party or the person alleged to have negligently caused the injury. Many people believe that the third-party carrier will voluntarily pay the injured child's medical charges as they are incurred. But that rarely happens. If there is evidence to show that the insured person was at fault for the incident that gave rise to the child's injury, the third-party carrier will usually make only one payment to settle the entire claim. But oftentimes settlement should be resisted until the full extent of the child's injuries is known. This is because the value of a case may depend on multiple factors, including the severity of the injuries, the duration of recovery, the need for future treatment, and whether the injuries are permanent. Depending on the extent of the injuries, it may take many months or even years to provide the answers to those questions.

A first-party insurance company is one that is contractually obligated to provide benefits to its insured or family members of the insured. One example of a first-party insurer is the parents' private health insurance carrier. Most parents already know that they can submit bills through a private health insurance policy, which one or both parents may have through their employer. In the case of an automobile accident, the child may have access to "no-fault" medical benefits under a policy issued to one of the parents (assuming that the child is a passenger in the vehicle). The term "no-fault" means that the coverage is available regardless of whether or not the claimant was at fault for the accident.

In Washington, these "no-fault" medical benefits are provided under coverage known as Personal Injury Protection (PIP). An auto insurance carrier must offer PIP coverage to the policyholder unless that policyholder rejects this coverage in writing. PIP coverage also compensates for lost wages and domestic help that may be necessitated by the person's injuries. However, these benefits usually do not come into play when the claimant is an injured child. The minimum coverage mandated under a PIP policy is $10,000. The maximum amount of coverage for PIP benefits is $35,000.

In the case of a pedestrian accident in which a child has been hit and injured by a motor vehicle, most people are unaware that the child may also have access to the driver's PIP coverage. Washington law requires the PIP carrier to offer these benefits to any pedestrian who has been injured by a motor vehicle. It does not matter if the pedestrian was at fault for the incident. If the child's parents also have PIP, this is another source of coverage if the at-fault driver's PIP coverage is exhausted.

In the case of a premises liability insurance policy, like a homeowner's policy, a child may have access to "no-fault" medical benefits. These policies will usually provide coverage if the child was injured on the premises and there is an insurance policy in place. For example, a child who slips and falls in a person's home should have access to no-fault medical benefits under the homeowner's insurance policy. The same is usually true if the injury occurred in a commercial business. These no-fault medical benefits are often limited and coverage may not exceed $5,000 to $10,000.

Local and State Assistance Programs

Children have access to benefits through Washington's Department of Social and Health Services (DSHS). DSHS is a state agency that administers many public benefits and services programs (visit www1.dshs.wa.gov). DSHS is divided into many different departments which administer these benefits. One of these departments is the Division of Developmental Disabilities (DDD) which coordinates state-funded services for individuals with disabilities. DDD coordinates medical benefits and arrangement of personal care through Medicaid. The DSHS Infant Toddler Early Prevention Program coordinates early intervention services for families with children ages 0 to 3 who have developmental delays. The Mental Health Division of DSHS contracts with support networks to provide community-based mental health services.

DSHS and DDD also host a number of specialized benefit programs to serve disabled adults who were injured prior to age 18. These include case management, supervised housing, and adult day programs. DSHS's Department of Vocational Rehabilitation (DVR) has programs to assist with adult education and training, housing, and in-home nursing.

Federal Assistance Programs

Many of the federal programs available to people with disabilities are partially or totally based on the assets owned by, or available to, the individual. The majority of programs offered are generated through, or in conjunction with, funding available under the Social Security Act. There are four basic disability-rated benefit programs.

Social Security Retirement Benefits (SSA) and Supplemental Security Income (SSI) are two programs that provide income assistance. SSA provides income to workers who have made the requisite contributions to the system through payment of FICA taxes. SSI may provide a guaranteed minimum income to a disabled person who has not made adequate contributions to a personal Social Security account. Eligibility for SSI is based on disability requirements and financial need. A child under the age of 18 can qualify for SSI benefits if the child meets Social Security's definition of disability for children, and if the child's income and resources fall within the eligibility limits. But the income of other people in the child's household are also considered when determining the child's financial need. The amount of the SSI payment differs from one state to another because some states supplement the SSI payment.[38] The eligibility criteria for children may be tough to meet based on Social Security's stringent financial requirements and its definition of disability.

Medical assistance is available under Medicare, but eligible participants must be eligible for SSA benefits. Medicare provides only listed hospital and doctors' services. Medicaid is another federally funded program, but it is a state-administered program. Eligibility for Medicaid is based on SSI criteria for both disability and need.

The Social Security Act also authorizes the State Children's Health Insurance Program (SCHIP). Families who earn too much to qualify for Medicaid may qualify for SCHIP. For little or no cost, families who earn less than $37,000 per year can purchase insurance so the child will have access to doctor, hospital, immunization, and emergency room services. The Washington state coordinator for SCHIP is:
Kevin Cornell, Designee

---

38. See www.ssa.gov.

Division of Eligibility and Service Delivery
Health and Recovery Services Administration
Department of Social & Health Services
805 Plum Street, NE, Mail Stop 45534
Olympia, WA 98504-5534
Email: corneke@dshs.wa.gov
Telephone: 360-725-1423

School Resources

Education is a basic constitutional right in Washington State.[39] Students have certain rights and responsibilities, and school districts have certain legally defined duties. Students cannot be denied educational opportunities because of race, origin, *disability*, pregnancy, or juvenile court involvement. With respect to disabled students, school districts have an obligation to provide special education and services to those students who qualify. A district may also be required to "reasonably accommodate" a student's disabilities even though the student does not need specialized instruction. A child with a learning disability is typically defined as a child with a mental, physical, or emotional impairment that affects the child's ability to learn. A child who experiences impairment from an orthopedic injury or from a traumatic brain injury will usually meet the criteria of a learning disability.

All children under the age of 22 who have a learning disability or impairment are eligible for additional services and support to help them achieve a meaningful education. An important federal law that achieves this purpose is the Individuals with Disabilities Education Act (IDEA). Washington specifically adopted the provisions of the IDEA as of July 2007. Another important law is Section 504 of the Rehabilitation Act, which prohibits discrimination against disabled students in programs

---

39. The Washington Constitution states that an ample education is the state's paramount duty. The state has an important duty to provide a system of public education for students of school age. See Wash. Constitution, Art. 9, §1 and §2.

receiving federal funds, such as public schools. Both of these laws require public schools in Washington to meet the educational needs of children with disabilities.

In Washington, school districts have an affirmative duty to identify all students who might need special education services. But from speaking to childcare experts, I have learned that most districts do a very poor job of this. There are many children who "fly under the radar" and are not properly identified as candidates. Washington law requires a special education evaluation of the child if the parent requests it. A parent should make the request in writing to the school principal and keep a copy for his or her records. The request should be made for both a special education evaluation under the IDEA and Section 504 (in case the child may not meet the eligibility requirements under the IDEA). The letter should also describe all problems the parent believes the child is having, since this may affect the degree or comprehensiveness of the testing. Once the written request is received, the school must meet certain conditions in specific time periods.

In making its evaluation, the district must review the child's medical and education records in the school files or those provided to it by the child's parent. The child's parent can also have an impact by checking in periodically with the school until the evaluation is completed. The evaluation must cover all areas in which a disability is suspected. These areas may include the child's physical and mental health, vision, hearing, social and emotional health, general intelligence, academic performance, communication (speech and language), and motor abilities.

The district's evaluation will be done by a professional, such as a school psychologist. If the evaluation must be accomplished by outside experts, the district must pay for this expense. If the parent disagrees with the evaluation, he or she can discuss it with school personnel, request mediation, file a complaint, or request a due process hearing in accordance with the IDEA or Section 504. Upon request, the district must also provide a parent with information regarding where to go for an independent evaluation by someone not associated with the district.

After an evaluation, the district will create an Individualized Education Program (IEP). The IEP is a detailed description of the instruction and services the disabled child will need to obtain a meaningful education. The child's parents must agree to the IEP plan before it can be implemented.

The IEP will have measurable goals and ways of monitoring the student's progress. More than one person or professional may be involved with creating the IEP, also called the IEP Team. Parents can be a part of the IEP Team. A parent who is a member of the IEP Team can also invite other people to join who may be effective advocates for the child (e.g., child's therapist, doctor). The IEP is good for one year, and can be modified in subsequent years. *The IEP must be provided to and implemented on behalf of the student **at no cost to the student or parents**.*

In Washington, students in grades K through 9 with learning difficulties who are not eligible for special education assistance may be eligible for special assistance through the state's Learning Assistance Program (LAP). The LAP is designed for students who do not meet the state's learning standard for that grade level. Again, parents should ask the school principal about the child's eligibility for the district's LAP and what services may be offered.

Usually a parent will need to take assertive action with the child's school to make sure the child has access to all available resources the school must provide under the law. If there is one common theme that I see in child injury cases, it is that many schools do a poor job of spotting children who may have a disability and then completing an appropriate evaluation so that the child's needs are taken care of. An informed parent, who properly communicates with school officials (in writing) and then follows up to make sure the school is fulfilling its legal obligation, can have an enormous impact.

Other Resources for Parents and/or Children

Here is a list of other resources that may be helpful to children with disabilities and their parents and/or family members.

- **Office of the Family and Children's Ombudsman (OFCO)**
6720 Fort Dent Way, Suite 240
MS TT-99
Tukwila, WA 98188
(800) 571-7321
http://www.governor.wa.gov/ofco/contact.asp

The OFCO ensures that government agencies respond appropriately to children in need of state protection, children residing in state care, and families under state supervision due to findings or allegations of child abuse or neglect.

- **Office of the Education Ombudsman (OEO)**
1110 Capitol Way South, Suite 304
PO Box 40004
Olympia, WA 98504-0004
(866) 297-2597
http://www.governor.wa.gov/oeo/

The OEO was created to assist elementary and secondary public school students and families in Washington. The OEO can help families understand how the public school system works, how to find education-related resources, and how to resolve conflict with schools. Complaints can also be filed with the OEO.

- **Catholic Family and Child Service**
5301 Tieton Drive, Suite C
Yakima, WA 98908-3478
(800) 246-2962
www.ccyakima.org

This organization administers a Transitional Living Program to youth between the ages of 18-21, offering assistance and mentoring to help establish housing, employment or training, and basic educational requirements.

• TeamChild[40]
Main Office-King County
1225 South Weller Street, Suite 420
Seattle, WA 98144
(206) 322-2444
www.teamchild.org

TeamChild is a nonprofit legal advocacy program for youth. It advocates for high-risk youth, helping to access their rights to education, mental and medical health benefits, and safe living situations.

• Parents are Vital in Education (PAVE)
Tacoma PAVE (main office)
6316 South 12th Street, PMB # 482
Tacoma, WA 98465
(253) 565-2266
(800) 5-PARENT (V/TTY)
www.washingtonpave.com

PAVE conducts workshops and training for parents on special education and related issues. PAVE helps parents increase skills in working with their children's teachers, therapists, and other team members to obtain appropriate educational services for students with disabilities.

---

40. TeamChild offers the Education Advocacy Manual that can be downloaded for free from their Web site. Information in this chapter concerning school resources was gleaned from this manual.

- **Within Reach** (formerly Healthy Mothers, Health Babies)
11000 Lake City Way NE, Suite 301
Seattle, WA 98125
(206) 284-2465
www.withinreachwa.org

Within Reach maintains current information on public and private early intervention resources, including Family Resource Coordinators. It also provides services and information about immunizations, nutrition, and other children's health services available in Washington State.

- **Children and Adults with Attention Deficit/Hyperactivity Disorder (CHADD)**
8181 Professional Place, Suite 150
Landover, MD 20785
(800) 233-4050, (301) 306-7070
(301) 306-7090 FAX
www.chadd.org

CHADD is a national nonprofit organization for children and adults with ADD/ADHD. CHADD is dedicated to improving the lives of people with ADD/ADHD through support, education, and advocacy. There are 12 CHADD Chapters in the state of Washington.

- **Advocates for the Rights of Citizens with Developmental Disabilities (The Arc)**
2600 Martin Way E, Suite B
Olympia, WA 98506
(360) 357-5596, (888) 754-8798
(360) 357-3279 FAX
www.arcwa.org

The Arc of Washington State is a nonprofit organization whose mission is to promote education, self-sufficiency, self-advocacy, and inclusion of individuals with developmental disabilities and their families. There are 11 local Arc Chapters throughout the state of Washington.

• Federation of Families for Children's Mental Health (FFCMH)

Federation of Families
9605 Medical Center Drive, Suite 280
Rockville, MD 20850
(240) 403-1901
(240) 403-1909 FAX
www.ffcmh.org

FFCMH is a national organization that serves the needs of children with serious emotional, behavioral, and mental disorders, and their families. The FFCMH responds to mail, telephone, in-person, and electronic inquiries by providing publications, information on seminars, workshops, speaker's bureaus, and crisis intervention and support groups.

• National Dissemination Center for Children with Disabilities (NICHCY)

PO Box 1492
Washington, DC 20013
(800) 695-0285 (V/TTY)
(202) 884-8441 FAX
www.nichcy.org

NICHCY provides information on resource sheets that identify organizations and agencies within each state that address disability-related issues. Resource sheets include agencies that serve children and youth with disabilities, state chapters of disability organizations, parent groups, and parent training and information projects.

• Learning Disabilities Association of Washington (LDAW)
16225 NE 87th Street, Suite B-4
Redmond, WA 98052
(425) 882-0820, (800) 536-2343

LDAW provides a variety of services focused on the education and general welfare of children and adults who have learning disabilities, attention deficit disorders, and related behavioral and social difficulties. LDAW offers tutoring for children and adults with learning disabilities. There is a sliding scale fee for tutoring.

Chapter Twelve

The Benefits of Hiring a Lawyer

If you have carefully read the previous chapters about the many different legal requirements and nuances involved in children injury claims, it may not take much effort to convince you that hiring an experienced lawyer is a smart move. There are too many things that can go wrong when handling a claim on behalf of an injured child. You want to hire someone who is a professional and who has years of experience dealing with insurance companies. Remember, the insurance company will be doing everything it can to minimize the claim and avoid paying fair compensation to cover the child's past expenses and future needs. Don't help the adjustor by going it alone; give serious thought to hiring an experienced attorney to handle your child's injury claim, especially when the injuries are serious or permanent.

Whether a Lawyer is Necessary

How do you know if a lawyer is necessary? Not every case requires a lawyer. And there are no hard and fast rules about whether a given case needs a lawyer. Generally speaking, the child usually has to have suffered a fairly serious injury caused by another party's negligence. Sometimes the negligence may be easy to spot, such as when the injury was caused by a negligent driver. Other times it may not be easy to spot and more investigation may be necessary. An example may be a highway design case or a premises liability case.

Usually the child's injuries have to be severe enough to justify the expense of hiring a lawyer and the costs associated with pursuing a claim (e.g., expert costs, records expense). Again, there are no hard and fast rules, but if the child's injuries resolve after a few months, the case may not be serious enough to justify the expense of a lawyer. Of course, there are exceptions, like those cases involving significant scarring or disfigurement.

For instance, a dog bite injury may only result in low hospital and medical charges (less than a few thousand dollars), but the incident may leave a prominent scar on the child's face that could affect the child for many years to come. In that situation, the child's case may warrant the services of an experienced attorney because the total overall value of the claim may be in the low- to mid-five figures, or even higher depending on the existence of other factors. Again, each case is different and will depend on the facts involved. When in doubt, parents should at least consult with an experienced lawyer to learn more about the child's rights and to determine whether the expense of an attorney is justified in a particular case.

Contingency Fee

Understandably, most people are wary of hiring an attorney because of the expense. Cases involving injury claims are usually handled by experienced lawyers on a contingency basis. With a contingent fee agreement, the lawyer agrees to defer his or her fee until the case successfully resolves. The fee is based on a percentage of the recovery obtained by the lawyer. If there is no recovery, then no attorney fee is owed. Most contingency fees can range anywhere from 25% to 50% of the recovery.

Often a serious accident case involving a child can take years to resolve and the lawyer will spend hundreds of hours on the case before he or she gets paid. The riskier and more complex the case, the higher the contingency fee will be. If a lawyer takes on a case that has a high risk of failure, and hence the possibility of receiving no fee, that lawyer will usually want a higher contingency fee as a premium for taking on the risk of not getting paid. Contingency fees allow people of limited financial resources to hire the best legal representation possible. This helps to level the playing field because the insurance companies usually retain some of the most expensive and experienced defense attorneys to help deny, delay, and defend the claim.

The costs associated with a claim are a different matter. The term "costs" refers to those expenses that are incurred while investigating the claim and, if necessary, prosecuting it in court. Examples of typical costs include expert fees, court costs, deposition fees, and record retrieval expenses. In Washington, an attorney is permitted to advance all costs and then deduct them from the client's recovery at the conclusion of the case. This allows the client to hire an attorney without ever having to pay out of pocket. Most experienced and reputable accident attorneys will agree to advance costs in a case. There are exceptions, of course, depending on the type of case and the facts involved.

What a Good Lawyer Can Do For You

Many people do not know what an experienced lawyer can do in these types of cases. Here is a list of the types of services that the lawyer may provide:

- Conduct initial interview with parents and/or child.
- Educate and teach parents and/or child about the claim process.
- Educate and teach parents and/or child about the court approval and Settlement Guardian ad Litem process.
- Educate and teach parents about the litigation process.
- Draft and file petition to appoint the Settlement Guardian ad Litem (SGAL).
- Gather written records and documents to support the claim, including medical records, school records, police report, etc.
- Perform investigation of the child's claim, including gathering witness statements, photographs, diagrams, and

physical evidence.

- Read and analyze applicable insurance policies that may apply (e.g., auto, homeowners, health) to see what coverage is available to pay for the child's damages, like medical, hospital, and wage loss benefits.
- Meet and confer with the child's medical doctors and other healthcare providers to fully understand the child's condition.
- Meet and confer with the SGAL to discuss the case and provide all relevant information regarding the child's claim.
- Obtain specific reports from experts to support the child's claim.
- Analyze any pertinent legal issues that may affect the child's case, such as contributory negligence, assumption of risk, comparative fault, etc.
- File necessary claim forms with the at-fault governmental agency.
- Analyze health insurance or governmental benefit plan to ascertain whether any money spent by either entity on behalf of the child must be repaid.
- Analyze and address any liens asserted against the settlement recovery. (Various healthcare providers, insurers, governmental agencies may file liens seeking to be repaid money for benefits already paid to or on behalf of the child.)
- Assist parents in locating available resources to assist with the child's recovery (local, state, federal, and nonprofit assistance programs).
- Contact the insurance company about the claim and conduct periodic discussions with the carrier about the case so that appropriate reserves are set aside to settle it.
- Conduct negotiations with the insurance adjustor in an effort to settle the claim, either prior to litigation or trial.
- If a lawsuit will be filed, prepare and draft the summons and complaint to file in court.

- Perform an investigation to locate the defendant so that personal sevice of the summons and complaint can be achieved.
- Arrange for personal service of the summons and complaint on the defendant as required by law.
- Prepare and draft written questions for information from the other side (called *interrogatories* and *requests for production*).
- Prepare the parents and/or child for deposition.
- Prepare for and conduct the deposition of the defendant and other lay witnesses.
- Discuss and/or meet the child's teachers to assist in understanding the effect of the child's injuries and need for educational resources.
- Meet with the child's physicians to prepare for their own deposition when requested by the defense attorney.
- Prepare to take the deposition of the defendant's experts, including medical experts.
- Prepare the parents and child for the child's medical examination by the defendant's medical experts.
- Answer questions and produce information and records requested by the other side.
- Review and analyze the child's medical records and billings.
- Hire other necessary experts to support or prove the claim, including other physicians, economists, engineers, vocational experts, etc.
- Review and analyze expert reports about the case, including those addressing liability, injuries, and damages.
- File the necessary documents in court as required by the judge, including witness lists, trial readiness, settlement conferences, etc.
- Prepare the parents, child, and other witnesses for trial.
- Create and prepare exhibits for trial.
- Organize records and other documentary evidence intended to be introduced at trial.

- Prepare for mediation and/or arbitration by organizing records and other documents for submission to the mediator or arbitrator.
- Research and write briefs and file motions to keep out or let in certain evidence at trial.
- Perform or participate in mock trials or focus groups to prepare for trial.
- Try the case over the course of several days before a judge or jury.
- Analyze verdict and research any issues that occurred at trial.
- Write briefs or motions following the verdict to obtain post-trial relief, including motions for attorney fees, or to overturn the verdict.
- Analyze trial record to determine if an appeal is warranted.
- Research and write briefs and motions if an appeal is filed.
- Negotiate subrogation claims submitted by a third party (the child's insurance company, or a government agency) that has the right to be paid back out of the settlement recovery for benefits previously paid to or on behalf of the injured child.
- Review and analyze the SGAL's report regarding the recommendation to approve or reject the child's settlement.
- Draft and prepare the petition asking the court to approve the minor child's settlement.
- Attend and argue the court hearing regarding the approval of the minor child's settlement.
- If a blocked account is to be opened for the child, provide the financial institution with necessary information.
- If an annuity is to be purchased, provide the furnisher of that annuity with all necessary information and complete all necessary paperwork, release forms, disclosure statements, etc.
- If a trust fund is to be created for the benefit of the child, review and complete all necessary paperwork, release forms, disclosure statements, etc.

- Draft and file in court the appropriate written proof or receipts showing creation of the blocked account, annuity purchase, or managed trust account.

This is a general list of various tasks that the lawyer may need to be complete in any given case. There may be additional tasks, depending on the facts of the case and the child's needs. This list will, at least, give the reader some idea of the type of work that may be necessary to successfully pursue a legal claim on behalf of an injured child.

Chapter Thirteen
Why I Wrote this Book

I have been representing adults and children in injury accident cases for nearly fifteen years. I have devoted my entire law practice to accident and injury claims. That's all I do. So if you want a lawyer to help you with a divorce or a business problem or some type of real estate transaction, I can't help you.[41] As I explained in prior chapters, there are special considerations involved in child injury cases. I've encountered too many situations where the insurance company took advantage of the child or the child's parents, or the parents made some serious mistakes, resulting in a settlement amount that was far less than what I would describe as reasonable.

Parents who find themselves in the terrible position of having to handle an injury claim for their child deserve to have sound information about the claims process and how to deal with the insurance company. They should have enough information to help them find and hire a good reputable injury lawyer for their child's case if one is needed. The decision to hire an attorney is an important one. The lawyer a parent chooses can have a tremendous influence on the outcome of the child's case. In some situations, the lawyer hired by the parent can have long-lasting consequences—good and bad.

Finally, parents never want to think of their child being injured or killed, and thus they are never prepared when this happens. When a child is seriously injured, everything changes. Parents may suddenly be forced to take care of the child's

---

41. If you live in the state of Washington, call us for a referral to another type of attorney. I have relationships with good attorneys in many different specialties. My office does not charge for this service.

medical and legal needs. This can be an overwhelming experience that no parent will ever want to encounter. Hopefully this book has provided some measure of solace and awareness for those parents who must now consider the legal questions and issues that must be addressed. In the end, I wrote this book because I am a parent myself. And I know firsthand what a parent may go through when that parent's child is seriously harmed by the negligence of another. I want this book to help that parent do what he or she is likely already doing-protecting and advancing the best interests of the child.

ABOUT THE AUTHOR

Washington attorney Christopher Michael Davis has been representing children and adults in accident cases and against insurance companies since 1994. In 2006, he was named a ***Rising Star Attorney*** by *Washington Law & Politics* magazine (this recognition is given only to the top 2.5% of lawyers age 40 and under in Washington State). In 2007 and 2008, *Washington Law & Politics* named Mr. Davis a ***Super Lawyer*** (recognizing the top 5% of *all* lawyers in Washington). Recently, Mr. Davis was named one of the "Top 100 Trial Lawyers" in the state of Washington by the American Trial Lawyers Association.

Mr. Davis speaks at Continuing Legal Education seminars on topics related to personal injury. He teaches and instructs other lawyers in Washington State on topics such as jury selection, proving damages, and developing winning trial techniques.

Mr. Davis has been licensed to practice law in Washington State since 1993. He has obtained millions of dollars in verdicts and settlements for his clients. He has successfully represented numerous children in serious accident cases involving traumatic brain injury, paralysis, and wrongful death. Mr. Davis is a member of numerous professional organizations, including the Washington State Trial Lawyers Association, American Association for Justice, and the North American Brain Injury Society.

For a sampling of verdicts and settlements achieved by Mr. Davis in a variety of cases, please visit his firm's Web site at www.DavisLawGroupSeattle.com.

WA